of related interest

Approaches to Case Study
A Handbook for Those Entering the Therapeutic Field
Robin Higgins
ISBN 1 85302 182 2

Approaches to Research
A Handbook for Those Writing a Dissertation

Robin Higgins

Jessica Kingsley Publishers
London and Bristol, Pennsylvania

The right of Robin Higgins to be identified as author of this work has been asserted by him in accordance with the Copyright, Designs and Patents Act 1988.

First published in the United Kingdom in 1996 by
Jessica Kingsley Publishers Ltd
116 Pentonville Road
London N1 9JB, England
and
1900 Frost Road, Suite 101
Bristol, PA 19007, U S A

Copyright © 1996 Robin Higgins

Library of Congress Cataloging in Publication Data
Higgins, Robin, 1925–
Approaches to research / Robin Higgins.
p.   cm.
Includes bibliographical references and index.
ISBN 1-85302-307-8 (alk. paper)
1. Psychotherapy--Research. I. Title.
RC337.H54   1996
616.89'14'072--dc20   96-32048
                                                                         CIP

British Library Cataloguing in Publication Data
A CIP catalogue record for this book is available from the British Library

ISBN 1-85302-307-8

Printed and Bound in Great Britain by
Cromwell Press, Melksham, Wiltshire

Contents

Boxes

Acknowledgements

In the preparation of this book, I am deeply grateful to Jessica Kingsley; to Alison Feess-Higgins, Ian Higgins, Nancy Lindisfarne, and Marietta Marcus; to staff and students at the Laban Centre for Movement and Dance; and to many others who have contributed indirectly, after their own fashion.

The Objectives of This Book Are:

1. To assist you in planning a research dissertation, thesis, treatise, project (throughout this book these terms are used synonymously) of 5000 words or more.

2. To introduce you to some of the main features in qualitative and quantitative research approaches and designs.

3. To enhance your understanding of the current literature on research.

Finding Our Bearings

1. What do you mean by research?

2. What do you mean by qualitative and quantitative approaches?

3. Do you equate research and science? Do you relate the two at all?

4. What do you see as the relation between science, logic, and maths?

5. What do you see as the relation between science and art? Science and religion?

6. As an artist or religious believer, do you hold views that confirm or conflict with a scientific attitude? Can you envisage ways of settling any such conflict?

7. How would you tackle superstition? Credulity? Fraud?

8. Do you value scepticism?

CHAPTER I

The Idiom of Research

Research is an act with an objective. The act entails a person (the researcher) searching for, enquiring about, investigating, exploring, repetitively, carefully, closely, some specified matter (the topic, the subject of the research). This matter may be an event, a fact, a cause, a relation, an elucidation, a demystification, a pattern, a meaning. So in any research:

a person   searches for   a clue

The word research is akin to the French word *recherche* with all its associations to Proust's memorable work: *A la Recherche du Temps Perdu* (the re-search for lost time).

Besides the search itself, there is the context in which the search is conducted. In one sense, research and practice should go together; a circular process. (See for example Lewith and Aldridge 1993 p.93 on the scientist-practitioner model in complementary medical research). Different types of practice may mean different types of research. But each feeds the other. This mutual enhancement of research and practice is one basic idea which underlies this book. Research should be part of your *curriculum vitae* in the broadest use of that term.

There is, however, a narrower use of the term which links *curriculum vitae* with professional advancement. Here research takes on a 'cachet' element. What has he or she written? How will their writings affect the status of this institution? The search for the cachet may profoundly affect the questions we ask, the topics we choose, and the way we go about developing and implementing them. Who are the important gate-keepers I have to influence by my research? To whom will this topic appeal? For various reasons, including mercenary pressures, the search may become a compulsive presentation of papers, with depressing effects on researcher and quality of research alike. (See further Altman 1994 and Barlow 1992.) The question of the funding of projects by parties that might have an interest in the slant of the results carries additional complex implications for the 'cachet' element in research. (See further Smith 1994b on academic integrity.) The student needs to be constantly aware of this 'cachet' element, though I will say little more about it in this book.

When we begin our research, we begin a journey of exploration where our steps may move outwards into the world about us, or, inwards into our memories and experiences or, more usually, in both directions simultaneously or successively. The subject may shape the object and *vice versa*. A central theme in research concerns this relation between experimenter and experiment.

Research is a journey where we may discover what, through our imagination, we anticipated, as when we test a hypothesis and find it holds for the moment. Research may also be a journey where the events and relationships we are investigating take a turn we never expected. We are overwhelmed by surprise. Our cherished beliefs and stereotypes are shattered. We are like an author who comes upon characters in the novel he's writing that he never knew were there.

> A music therapist was conducting an observational case-series study into the effects of music on a group of patients with Alzheimer's disease. He noticed the striking effect that recalling a childhood nursery rhyme had on one particular patient. In this 72-year-old woman, remembering the tune and then the words of the nursery rhyme acted like a Winnicottian transitional object, re-focusing her consciousness and bringing her back into the present. She was like someone coming out of coma. The therapist re-orientated his dissertation from an experimental study involving several cases to a phenomenological single case-report, which he entitled: 'Retrieving the inner child through auditory memory'. What started in the world of prose, he said, fetched up as poetry. 'It was quite a surprise.'

(The examples and vignettes in this book are designed for teaching purposes. To this end, and for reasons of confidentiality, the details of people and events including the titles of any dissertation, though rooted in actuality, have been altered and in that sense turned into fiction.)

Scepticism, credulity and fraud

Another underlying theme in research is the scepticism that may usefully be developed towards everything we confront in or outside of ourselves. We need to be perpetually open to a new look. Only a large measure of scepticism can tear away the veils that hide from us the truth that many of the things we do are done for motives and with viewpoints very different from those we believe we hold or claim to hold (Russell 1935, p.25).

We need our intuitions derived from a casestudy to set up hypotheses which we can then be sceptical about. A basic tenet of the research approach demands that we question every statement that we make. What do we mean exactly by this term or that proposition? Are our definitions, propositions, models, so unambiguous that others such as fellow researchers know exactly what we mean? Are our hypotheses so formulated that we or others can prove them false or not?

This mantle of logical scepticism, which we have to put on when we undertake research, can be exciting or disturbing or both. No one finds it easy to have their everyday assumptions questioned and sometimes turned topsy-turvy. Who is going to relish having their more extravagant flights of fancy cut short by prosaic and persistent rational probing? The combination of intuitive flights and their sceptical examination is hard to sustain. That is one reason, an understandable one, why the term 'research' is apt to pitch students into panic even if they have had some basic scientific training.

But in this respect, research is no different from any other reflexive exercise, such as the questioning of techniques, assumptions, habits, rituals, or simply why we do this rather than that. The reluctance we often experience over starting on such exercises may help to explain our reluctance to start on research.

Credulity is a readiness to believe, in particular a readiness to believe on weak or insufficient grounds.

EXERCISE ONE

A salesman confronts you outside a chemist's shop in the High Street. He has a card on which are stuck a row of small round paper markers. He presses you to allow him to pin one of these markers on the back of your hand. 'It registers your degree of stress' he says. When it's blue, it means you're very relaxed. When it turns through green to brown and silver, it means you're becoming increasingly stressed. He tells you to keep the marker on all day and make a note of when and how the colour changes. While you're in the shop, the marker records a deep blue. As you walk through the streets to a picture gallery, sure enough as he predicted ('negotiating traffic may cause you to become stressed') it changes colour, through green to brown. You're not however aware of any upsurge of anxiety. Once you are inside the gallery, and gazing at the Impressionists, your marker returns to its original deep blue.

What sort of questions might you put to the salesman?

Hint: Some of them might be the sort of questions you would ask when assessing the use of a Lie Detector in the courts. (For suggested answers see p.105.)

In one sense, the history of discovery may be read as a reduction or realignment of our credulity. From an enlightened viewpoint (and some would say that in itself is invested with considerable credulity), the history of discovery reflects the correction of our misperceptions (the flat earth), misconceptions (the earth-centred universe), superstitions, and the many other mistakes in 'knowledge' that have clouded our ability to dis-cover nature.

One outcome of credulity is fraud, the deceit that may be practised, with different degrees of awareness, on us and by us. In research, the conscious or unconscious slanted selection of papers for publication, discussion, and review, the so-called 'bias of publication', is well recognized (see further Wheatley 1992). This is the tip of the iceberg. For a full study of fraud and misconduct in medical research in the UK and elsewhere see Lock and Wells 1993. Fraud feeds on credulity. Again from an enlightened viewpoint, the history of discovery may be read as the exposure of superstition and fraud.

Rycroft on his parents: 'I don't think it ever occurred to either of them that there was any conflict between science and religion; the enemy of both was superstition.' (Rycroft 1985, p.201)

The overall plan

When we start on a piece of work that may occupy us for at least six months, it's as well to take stock and have some overall plan. In this respect, the exercise does not differ from starting on any other enterprise. The observations that were made at the beginning of *Approaches to Case-Study* (see Higgins 1993) apply here with equal if not greater force. We may find ourselves constantly subjecting the details of any plan we make to revisions and alterations; the whole plan itself may be scrapped and replaced by another. The directions of the research, the topic and the methods we chose to study it, are bound to influence the shape of the plan, which is no more than a support for our ideas and arguments. The plan is a skeleton for our findings. But without a firm skeleton, buildings are apt to collapse. (For the use of word processing in laying out the headings of your plan, including database protocols and literary references, see Lewith and Aldridge 1993, Chapters 27 and 28.)

Preliminary questions you will need to ask

1. What is the topic of my thesis? What question(s) am I asking? What is the provisional title?

2. Why have I chosen this topic? What led me to it? How does it relate to me?

3. Why do I think this chosen topic is important? For local or global reasons?

4. How have other people approached this and related topics?

5. How am I going to cover the topic myself?

6. Have I tentatively envisaged any conclusions?

7. Who else is likely to be involved in my research? What ethical considerations and appropriate measures may need to be taken before I start?

In the layout of your thesis, the following suggested plan links these preliminary questions to later chapters in the book:

Box I: the overall plan for the dissertation

A. **An introduction**, in which you define **what** is the problem and the specified question(s) you are addressing, and outline the personal considerations that led you to it. **Why** did you start on this particular topic? (Questions 1–3 above and Chapter II).

B. **Methodology**, i.e. how are you going to study the problem? **How** are you approaching it? **How** are you translating this approach into action (research strategies and design)? (Questions 5 and 7 above and Chapters III and IV).

C. **A review of the literature**. (Questions 3 and 4 above and Chapter V). **What** have others found out about this particular topic?

D. **Your findings**. **What** did you find? what do your findings mean? **What** do they mean in relation to others' findings. (Question 5 and Chapter VI).

E. **Conclusions and synthesis**. **What** is the significance of your findings? **How** can they be used? **What** further possible steps do you envisage? **How** are you going to implement these? (Questions 3 to 6 above and Chapter VII).

F. **A short abstract of the whole exercise**. (Chapter VII).

Another way of thinking about the shape of the thesis is in terms of time:

1. What *has* happened so far in this topic? What *has* happened to bring me and the topic together? This is the historian's *retrospective* viewpoint.

2. What *is* happening in the process of my writing it? In the *here-and-now*? This is the world of interactive rhythms, well known to the counsellor and the arts therapist.

3. What is *going* to happen? The expected or unexpected part of the plan. This is the *prospective* view of, for example, the model-building scientist.

VIGNETTE (see note on p.2)

> In the middle of an improvising session with a group of three elderly patients, a music therapist remembered a short poem he'd written one night after reading an essay by Miroslav Holub on 'the dimension of

the present moment'. He called his poem 'the three second present' on the grounds that stimuli lasting more than three seconds cannot be held by our consciousness as a whole. The poem went like this:

I hold you

Past

To come.

Each line referred to an aspect of time: present, past, and future. Listening to his three patients, it occurred to the music therapist that it was not so far fetched to hear in each of their improvisations an echo of these three different aspects of time, touched on in his poem. One patient, a woman and the youngest of the group, would go back repeatedly to the start of her improvisation, reiterating and shortening the patterns, moving ever closer to her basic structures, her core motifs. Her music was distilling and contracting. Another was constantly moving in a new direction, as this grew out of the discarded one. Her music was groping forwards the whole time, restlessly expanding. The third member of the group took her cues from each of the other two in turn, and in this way, sought to stitch their musics together. Her music took on a static quality, contractions being balanced by expansions. That evening the music therapist started his thesis on 'Space–time in music therapy'.

Access

Question 7 on p.5 raises some important ethical issues, which you will need to resolve before going any further. If, in your proposed investigation, you will be using human subjects as part of an experimental design or simply as a source for your data, you will have to consider first the issues of confidentiality. These issues were described in *Approaches to Case-Study* (Higgins 1993, pp.11, 100, 110) as the bedrock on which the mutual trust between patient and professional is founded. Some of the controversies respecting confidentiality (such as informing police, insurance companies, even parents about their children) were listed. Confidential issues apply with even greater force in research, where there arises the possibility of publishing your findings. (For patients' rights in research see for example Warden 1991.)

Second you will have to observe the regulations governing official approval. Such approval may have to be obtained from your human subjects themselves, from the institution in which you are working with them, and from the institution in which you are studying. The regulations may vary according to the nature of the work and institutional context. In any event, you need to clarify these points before you start your dissertation, and confirm this clarification at some appropriate place under heading D in the overall plan.

The question of 'human subjects' is only one aspect of a wider issue to which you should give some thought before embarking on your research. Under the heading of Access, you need to clarify at least to yourself:

1. Whom you will be invited, requested, permitted, to see.

2. How confidential are these meetings; i.e. how widely may you disseminate your findings?

3. What are the boundaries involved in your access, and who are the gatekeepers with whom you will have to negotiate?

4. Who are likely to assist and who to block the later progress of your work? (See further in Hammersley and Atkinson 1993. Also Devish and Vervaeck 1986.)

> Gates can be put anywhere
>
> For someone to pass through
>
> And someone to keep.

The issue of access is an early occasion in which your research may become 'action research', i.e. research that entails social action, or that advances the social sciences through involvement in practical human problems and concerns (see further Miller 1993). Later occasions of such action research will include getting the dissertation accepted, published, and read, and getting your ideas disseminated, your suggestions implemented.

Guidelines

Finally, whilst in no way attempting to advise you on the actual writing of the thesis, (you will find many useful practical hints in Bell 1993 and Hall 1994), I suggest the following two guidelines may be of help. The first is concerned with *sticking to the topic*. Many students, from arts and science backgrounds alike, often experience some difficulty in sustaining the thread of an argument through the larger scale presentation of a dissertation. As you build up your material, you may find it useful, *from the start*, to remember subliminally that, whilst in the composition of your thesis there may be many routes to the final integrated product (the project may be assembled like a jigsaw or grow like a piece of knitting), *in the end* you will need to place every idea you introduce into some such hierarchy as the following:

Heading. (A–E above.)

Subsection. (Theme.)

Paragraph.

Sentence.

Key phrase.

Those readers who are musicians may recognize parallels with Arnold Schönberg's *Fundamentals of musical composition* (Schönberg 1970). The parallel is not insignificant. Arts therapy students will have practised stringing their ideas together, giving them a coherent and integrated form, in the medium of their choice be it music, painting, the dance, the drama. This practice may serve them in good stead when it comes to carrying out similar moves in the medium of written words.

Regard to this anatomy of levels (from heading through subsection, paragraph, sentence, and key phrase) will assist in achieving a second crucial feature of any dissertation: a sense of flow, of development. A good story has a beginning, middle, and end. Likewise, a good dissertation. Both should leave the reader with a strong feeling of having moved from A to B (or Z).

The movement may simply consist of coming out of a mist, of clarifying concepts which at the start were hazy. Or it may consist of analyzing concepts that at the start were over-simplified, or misguidedly clear. Or it may follow the conventional movement of rejecting the null hypothesis, and slotting in the next piece of a theoretical model.

Key phrases, in growing into sentences and paragraphs, generate their own momentum...like musical motifs.

EXERCISE TWO

Does *repetition* (Stravinsky's 'jumping up and down', the Red Queen's 'faster and faster' on the same spot) count as movement? (For some clues see p.105.)

CHAPTER II

The Introduction
Personal Background and Discovery

1. *What connections do you see between research, case study, and the expansion of your self through learning and discovery?*

2. *What events in your life have had a profound effect on you? How have these events and their effects influenced the questions that have intrigued you down the years? When did they happen? To whom did you address the questions? What sort of replies did you get? How did you deal with the replies? Was your curiosity satisfied? Are you one to persist until you are content with the answer? Or do you settle for what seems an inadequate reply and continue to work on it yourself? Were there occasions when you kept your questions entirely to yourself? If so, why?*

3. *What questions are on your mind at present? How do they relate to issues you feel strongly about?*

4. *Are the questions preoccupying you at present appropriate for research? If so, what form do you see this search taking? If you do not consider them appropriate, why is that? How might you change them to render them appropriate?*

5. *At home or at school, were you encouraged to ask questions? Who has struck you as genuinely interested in the questions you asked? With what results?*

6. *Have you found some questions pulled you off the course of your enquiry? Did the questions you asked cover up more salient questions you didn't ask? Was the encouragement to pursue the cover-up questions a subtle way of discouraging you from asking the more salient ones?*

7. *Have there been times when, on reflection, you can see that your act of asking questions was aimed at purposes other than to receive an answer? Did the person of whom you were asking the question spot these other purposes and deal with the 'questions' appropriately?*

The main tasks in the introduction are to state clearly:

(i) how and why you came to undertake this project.

(ii) the question(s) and topic(s) you are seeking to explore in it.

(iii) why it differs from what has gone before.

(i) How and why your project started

Questions, that carry meaning for us, grow out of experience. They often lead directly to a line of enquiry, a work setting, and a choice of research topic.

We can sometimes date the origin of a project to some particular occasion: a client who changed our outlook; an afternoon when we had a success or a disaster. The researcher's attention may be caught like a reader's by five opening gambits: an arresting story; a vivid scene; a strong quotation; an intriguing fact; an opinionated and controversial announcement (Albert 1992, p.39).

> It was a rainy Friday in November. She was the last person I was due to see. She was living on her own, had broken with her boyfriend, and saw little point in continuing to live. We sat for a while in silence looking out of the window into the dark as people were going home. Then without any suggestion on my part, she picked up a pencil and began to draw. We started a dialogue in visual images. That's when I became interested in the idea of what I later discovered was called the hermeneutical circle.

The origin may not always be so dramatic. Perhaps we read an article or a book and an idea slowly begins to germinate and get us going. The Introduction is not the place for a literature review, but a few pertinent references may be included to illustrate your topic, outline its significance, and show how your interests link with those of others.

We may consciously or unconsciously choose a line of research because of an event or set of events that had a profound effect on us: a bout of anorexia leads us to study anorexia; an occasion when we were physically abused leads us back to re-explore that experience.

> Hashim describes how as a young man of 17, two days before starting as a medical student, he temporarily blinded himself by watching an eclipse of the sun through smoked glass. The ophthalmologist he consulted compared the state of his patient's retina to a piece of paper pierced with a burning cigarette. The young man lived with despair for a few weeks, slowly recovered his sight, completed his medical training and specialized in ophthalmology. The persistent questions that preoccupied him in his later practice and that dated from this experience were:
>
> 1. What *possible* outcomes should we look for in any set of medical events?
>
> 2. By what ways can a doctor, selecting from this range of possible outcomes, keep hope alive in his patients? (Hashim 1994)

Or past experience may determine our research choice through a related symbol: a woman who was sexually abused as a child studies male domination and sado-masochism.

There is a constant circular connection between our experience and the questions we ask. Good writing comes from the heart. But if you are passionately engaged in a situation, you may not always find it easy to articulate immediately a cool and coherent question. To ask appropriate research questions, we need a degree of detachment and tranquillity. An initial sequence in the growth of any research project is:

An issue you feel strongly about ⟹ A coherent relevant question

(ii) Questions and topics

Questions

> The starting point for any research project is to ask a good question and develop a protocol laying out the methods that will be used to answer the question. (Oxman 1994)

Questions come in many guises. Here are four different types:

1. Content questions.

2. Process questions.

3. Check questions.

4. Distracting questions.

EXAMPLES

1. *Content questions*: where? who? what? where is Madagascar? what is twice two? what is the French for door? what is he doing? who is he? what does this image mean?

2. *Process questions*: how? why? what? how does this painting, piece of music, dance, 'work'? what effect is her behaviour having on me? how am I effecting a change? what are the steps in this change?

3. *Checking questions*: eg about efficiency (have I done what I set out to do?); authenticity (are my intentions honest?); alienation (what sort of trouble am I going to stir up?). (See further Reason and Rowan 1981, p.107–112.)

4. *Distracting questions*: who's going to win the next election? what am I going to give her for Christmas? did I turn off the gas?

The four types of questions are not mutually exclusive. According to context, a question may fall into any one of the four categories. But the distinctions are worth bearing in mind for the way they dovetail with choice of topic and research design. (See further Yin 1994.)

Sometimes a good question only arrives by repeatedly excluding other ones. We can often only reach a good question by trial and error. Perhaps too by retaining a degree of innocence, or by refusing to accept the received wisdom, like the child in the story of the Emperor's clothes (see further Kennedy 1991). Sometimes we can only appreciate the good question with hindsight, for example the question that stopped Fleming discarding the Petri dish and led to the discovery of the antibiotic powers of penicillin.

Good questions may arise through un-learning, as practised in psychotherapy and by all creatives. (See also 'un-history' in Higgins 1993, p.29.)

One crucial issue over questions involves unravelling those that are our own from those that are sown in our minds by others, by a prevailing mood in those around us, by a zeitgeist (see for example further projective identification in Hinshelwood 1989). In this connection, questions we ask may not reflect an authentic desire to know but more the role play of the conforming child, carrying out parental prescriptions. In undertaking 'cachet' research for professional advancement, we are particularly exposed to such questions.

Sometimes people manipulate our question asking. Situations arise in which one 'mustn't' ask questions: in a war, a hostile group, a totalitarian society. In ordinary times, the truth about ourselves, as Russell pointed out, is thought 'ill-mannered'; in war time, it is thought 'criminal' (Russell 1935, p.16). Arthur Miller in an article on censorship suggested 'that one of the main reasons the Soviet system collapsed was that the reality of Soviet life was forbidden to be examined...' (Miller A. 1994). Are your research questions bringing you up against the censor?

Questions (and question asking) may function as a cry for love, a weapon to pin down and/or annoy, a defence through distraction. Such questions, if unrecognized, lay a minefield for the researcher.

Two final points: finding the right question may be harder than answering it; and answering apparently simple questions may turn into the book that never ends.

EXERCISE THREE

> Consider what is implied in the following question: Does any arts therapy cure depression? (Some clues, p.106)

Topics

Different types of questions lead to different types of topics and different research strategies. In a case-study for example, the connections between question, topic, and research occur at several levels. We may first be puzzled by some feature which we want to clarify, interpret, or explain.

> An art therapy student was immediately struck by the appearance of a 'hairy clown' in an eight-year-old girl's painting. The student wanted to sift the meaning of this image, and started to keep a diary about the dialogue she had with the child, and both she and the child had with the image. This diary provided the core of her thesis. (See further in Chapter III, on hermeneutic research.)

Second, a case study may provide us with an example of a wider problem, which becomes the basis of our thesis.

A movement therapy student was struck by the peculiar movements of a ten-year-old boy in class and playground. The student made some enquiries and discovered the child had recently been involved in a fire at his home. The peculiar movements seemed to represent, in body language, one aspect of a post-traumatic stress disorder, which the student then made the topic for his thesis. (See further in Chapter III, on phenomenological research.)

Third, much of what applies to cases may apply to any of us who attempt to treat cases, or write theses about them. Our understanding of patients, any beneficial effect we may have on them, stem, to an important extent, from our ability to enter into their world, a world which for us is both the same and other. Entering this partly other world inevitably means expanding the boundaries of our own. This exercise of expansion entails a deep and intimate connection between case-study and research, a connection in which, for a while, researcher may merge with the subject of the research, and both emerge in an altered state.

A music therapy student in the course of an improvisatory session with a deeply disturbed patient found herself 'pulling back' into more formal musical structures, even resorting to musical clichés. She started to note carefully the contexts in which this formalization occurred, particularly its association with primitive images and violent feelings that erupted in herself and her patient. These notes became the main themes for her thesis on 'Containing madness in therapist and patient'. (See further in Chapter III, on heuristic research.)

EXERCISE FOUR: PERSONALITY, QUESTIONS, TOPICS AND TYPES OF RESEARCH

Different types of people ask different types of questions, and these in turn lead to different types of research. Thus there is a constant interplay between:

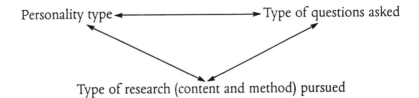

Personality type ← → Type of questions asked

Type of research (content and method) pursued

At this stage, you might find it worthwhile relating the type of questions that preoccupy you with the sort of person that you are, in order to give yourself some guidance on what sort of research you may feel most at home with, and what sort of changes in personality, type of question and research, you may be moving towards.

Some of the patterns in this three-fold connection, including the tensions that arise between them, have been described in Reason and Rowan 1981. Many systems have been devised for distinguishing personality types (for example Jung's typology and others outlined in Higgins 1993).

Types of topic

Topics take the form of propositions involving one or more issues, or units of analysis. (See further Yin 1994, p.23–4.) So topics may have to do with:

1. The FRAMES underlying the various therapeutic disciplines: personal and social settings; varieties of human resources and responses; posture/gesture; movements; the dance; painting/sculpting; drama; music; emotions; body-image; creativity. (Cf Content and process questions.)

2. Specific PROBLEMS arising within these frames and TECHNIQUES for tackling: for example diagnoses (depressions, alcoholism etc); improvisation; transference/counter-transference; multimedia techniques which combine music with painting, movement, drama. In action research, the focus is often on the social relationship as the instrument which effects change. (Cf Content and process questions.)

3. Accurate ASSESSMENT of therapeutic intervention: for example measuring change; measuring the effect of one identified variable on another; assessing the sensitivity and reliability of our research measures. (Cf Process and checking questions.)

These three headings are interrelated. A careful analysis of issues under heading 2 (problems and techniques) will often throw light on themes under heading 1 (frames). Freud and the depth psychologists showed how psycho-pathology may be an important way into psychology and anthropology, illustrating how, as Nietzsche said of Greek tragedy, one may turn diseases into great beneficial forces of culture (Nietzsche 1984 quoted in McNiff

1993). Similarly, the pursuit of accurate assessment leads to the setting up of testable models which in turn will throw light not just on the problems but also on the frames from which the problems arose.

Eliciting answers

The type of answers we receive in research depends on how we as researchers relate to the people who furnish us with our findings. Besides the actual questions we ask, there is the tone, the manner, the human dimension, the whole way we ask them.

Is the person we are addressing at any time in a mood or a setting to answer questions at all?

> In some situations one doesn't ask questions, because the person you ask may be constantly under fear of arrest and anyone asking questions may in some way precipitate that arrest. Also one doesn't ask because by asking you are revealing your own vulnerability. You should know, you shouldn't have to ask... (see further Agar 1980)

What sort of an immediate impression do we convey? In dress, authority, expertise, by our age, gender, ethnicity (see further on 'impression management' in Hammersley and Atkinson 1983). In presenting ourselves, how do we blend into the situation? How do we use such background knowledge as we may possess? To overwhelm, keep at bay? Or to draw into a sense of mutuality? Do we convey honesty or deception?

Are our questions directive, confrontational, prepared, the outcome of a planned approach? Or non-directive, arising out of what is said, following the trend of the conversation? In either event, we can expect different responses. The two types of questions, directive and non-directive, are likely to provide different kinds of data, and thus may be useful at different stages of the enquiry (Hammersley and Atkinson 1983, p.116. Also Yin 1994, p.84 on open-ended, or focused interviews and surveys).

Are we asking leading, weighted, persuasive questions? Or questions that assume a hidden agenda ('Have you left off beating your wife, answer yes or no?')?

> A 74-year-old lady with failing eyesight receives a letter and questionnaire from a survey organization. The letter informs her she's been selected at random to take part in a most important piece of

research sponsored by her local health authority. She will be helping the doctors improve their services. The letter assures her of the complete confidentiality with which her replies will be treated.

With the aid of a friend, she begins to fill out the ten-page form. When she reaches page five with questions about her sexual habits, she pauses: 'They must know who I am and where I live, else how did this thing reach me?' And then: 'They never asked me if I wanted to be involved'. And finally: 'How can it possibly help them improve their services by knowing that I have or haven't slept with members of my own sex?'

She tore the form up and heard twice more from this efficient organization. On the second occasion, they sent her another copy of the ten-page questionnaire in case she'd lost the first one.

The example illustrates how strict adherence to random sampling can result in an unrepresentative set of replies. More generally, it illustrates how a theoretically correct, statistically based approach, can founder in its practical human application. The point is of considerable moment in research and one to which we will return when we consider designs for large scale clinical trials. Here we need only note the ironic situation whereby, at times, the more we seek to exclude uncertainty from our house of reason, the more it slips in again through the back door. If, through basic problems over asking questions, the information at source is unreliable, the cleverest statistics are of little avail.

Mergence and e-mergence: two basic ways of finding out

Two drama therapists are having a debate about the *Tempest*.

> A: The point of the play is that it investigates the unique mind of Prospero. We are taken step by step into his world, with all its conflicts, resolutions, and internal logic.

> B: No, the point of the play is that it illustrates the divergences, the polarities of existence. You can't do that by drawing on the working of one mind.

A: We are invited into one person's meditation. That's all we can ever ask for. Certainly that's my understanding of meditation. Through emptying my mind, I dive deeper into the cosmos.

B: But the cosmos is outside myself just as the other characters in the *Tempest* are outside Prospero. Also meditation involves filling as well as emptying. What are you filling from?

A: The only thing we can ever be sure of is what goes on inside our own minds. Through the figure of Prospero, Shakespeare gives us a glimpse of what goes on in his own mind, as Plato did through the figure of Socrates.

B: But *we* can catch this glimpse. No man is an island. Shakespeare least of all. What he revels in is contrast and one basis for that contrast is what lies in his world and what in the world outside him.

We operate in an 'emic' mode when we identify or merge with the Other and reach 'synchronic' resonances, i.e. resonances taken at a single moment in time. We operate in an 'etic' mode when we retain a distance from the Other and reach 'diachronic' resonances, i.e. resonances taken over a period of time, allowing historical comparisons (see further Ruthven 1976, p.39. Pike 1967, Whitten and Hunter 1990, Seymour-Smith 1986, Hughes 1992).

Therapists will be familiar with these two contrasting but complementary states, though they may recognize them more easily through the dialectic of subjective mergence, objective e-mergence, and the synthesis of subjectively objective, objectively subjective, participant observer, neutral involvement. (See further Reason and Rowan 1981. Also Lewith and Aldridge 1993, p.93 and Heal and Wigram 1993, p.243.)

All research is underpinned by this complementarity of mergence and e-mergence. We use the complementarity in individual psychotherapy:

A patient was speaking about a difficulty she had falling asleep, and how she dealt with it by first turning on the television, and then the radio. Her counsellor, feeling his way into her difficulty and her way of dealing with it, was reminded of his own experiences when a child. His response had been the opposite of his patient's: far from filling his room with distracting noises, he had sought absolute quiet so that he could be sure of hearing the silence. But the contrast between their two responses enabled him to see the common ground: namely that what lay behind both his own and his patient's experience was a fear of the void, inherent in dropping off to sleep. She tried to fill this void with sounds; he, with silence.

We use the complementarity of mergence and e-mergence in improvisational techniques where what Bruscia describes as 'empathy' or 'intimacy' would fall under the heading of mergence; what he describes as 're-direction', would fall under the heading of e-mergence; and what he describes as 'structuring', 'elicitation', 'procedural', 'referential', 'discussion', would fall under the heading of the complementary dialogue between mergence and e-mergence (Bruscia 1987).

We use this same dialogue in certain approaches to organizational change:

> Two art therapists plan two related theses that look at the ways their work can be used most effectively across a number of day centres in a region. How can they catch a glimpse of how their colleagues in health, education, and the social services may feel towards the innovations the two therapists are proposing? How can they slip into the others' shoes (mergence)? How can they then detach themselves and tactfully communicate and implement their new proposals (e-mergence)?

Ethnography

A fourth instance of this complementarity between mergence and e-mergence may be found in ethnography, where we are concerned with making, reporting, and evaluating observations on customary behaviour in particular societies or cultures (Conklin 1968). The observations are derived from varying degrees of intimacy with these societies and may cover work with individuals or groups of different make-up and sizes. Ethnography has been described as 'highly particular and hauntingly personal...serving as a basis for grand comparisons and understanding within and across a society' (Van Maanen 1988).

EXERCISE FIVE

> Imagine yourself as an ethnographer in in a hospital. Can you envisage the different worlds that those around you inhabit? The patients' world? The worlds of the different teams that make up the staff? How do all these different worlds interrelate? (See further Atkinson 1992.)

The earliest ethnography was descriptions of unfamiliar cultural practices as recorded by explorers, missionaries, and staff on colonial government outposts. By the 19th century, more orderly methods and patterns of reporting were being developed. There was a steady shift from mere acceptance of reportage towards a more critical and craftsmanlike attention to its execution, and from a dominant concern with data accumulation to a deeper analysis of particular cultural patterns. Along with this shift went an appreciation of the need to:

1. Understand the local language (both verbal and nonverbal).

2. Define the cultural context and purpose of events described.

3. Dissect the role of the observer and the mode of observation.

4. Extend the techniques of observation (e.g. the use of films and sound-recordings along with psychological and sociological measuring instruments like projection tests, case studies, and surveys).

5. Derive forms of classification and standardization in order to organize the cross-indexing of data, and so move towards being able to distinguish cultural variability from cultural universals. (Cf The idea of ethnography as a system for understanding a historical culture in Vernant 1991.)

The ethnographer participates overtly or covertly in people's daily lives for an extended period of time, watching what happens, listening to what is said and asking questions. Ethnography is a unique type of natural history in which the observer becomes a part of and an active participant in the observed universe. Being such an intimate part of the world that is under study raises many questions that will be familiar to therapists. How does their own world view influence ethnographers in assessing someone else's? The central plank of therapists' training, their own analysis, is concerned with just such a question. Again, when ethnographers use themselves as research instruments par excellence (Hammersley and Atkinson 1993, p.180), are they not responding in a way that is analogous to the therapists' instrument of counter-transference?

From the significance attached to the observer/ethnographer, grows another key issue that will be familiar to therapists: how the right balance is struck between observer and participant; how to enjoy mutuality without taking over or being taken over by the other; how to retain a committed marginal stance, how to be a 'marginal native' (Hammersley and Atkinson 1993, p.100).

Through mergence and e-mergence, what we experience as alien in another person or situation, may sometimes cease to be. Our own world can connect with and understand another's. (See further under the hermeneutic approach pp.42–47).

The four instances given here of how we merge with and e-merge from those about us are drawn from successively larger populations. This is in keeping with the principle that concepts fashioned at first in a limited population, often stereotyped as psychopathological, may gradually come to be applied more generally. Through mergence and e-mergence, what was at first viewed as pathological becomes transformed and accepted into a larger system. Examples would be the 'de-pathologizing' of regression (where a breakdown becomes a breakthrough), projective identification, the paranoid-schizoid and depressive positions (see further Field 1994).

This transformation and enlargement works in a direction opposite to reductionism (that is, the attempt to explain a wide range of events (e.g. symptoms) by a solitary cause (e.g. Oedipal complex)). The transformation and its direction carries important implications for research.

(iii) How and why your project differs from what has gone before

In research, we invent a new look, or at least something we think is new; or we discover what was already there but wasn't recognized. It doesn't matter which. In either event, we come to terms with the Other: a key theme in any research. (For more about our relation with the Other, see the practical exercise in Higgins 1993, pp.12–3). A subsidiary theme is how we as researchers relate to our own research and the writing of it. Coleridge (see Chapter 5 in Harris Williams and Waddell 1991) defined two approaches to Otherness. He called them generating and fabricating. Without getting too involved with his philosophical system, we may set out the differences between these two approaches as follows:

Generating	Fabricating
Operates primarily through imagination.	Operates primarily on an intellectual level. Through fancy.
Shaping, transforming, unfolding images and ideas.	Piecing together, aggregating, rearranging bounded thoughts.
Organic growth.	Tends to the mechanical.
Einfall, associations.	Rote-memory.
The evolution of symbols, such as the killing of the albatross.	The manipulation of fixed forms, such as a set of four-line stanzas, to tell a story.
Living with incompatibles, including paradoxes ('life-in-death')	The resolution of paradoxes.
Sculpting a worldview over an unprescribable period. Tuning in to a slowly evolving self.	The attainment of testable goals within a prescribed period.

Though Coleridge set greater store by 'generating', both fabricating and generating are necessary for the successful completion of any piece of creative work. In writing your thesis, you will be fabricating when you undertake to produce it by a certain date, in a certain form, with so many words etc and when you employ 'fixed mechanisms' such as the Harvard system for references.

You will be generating when you allow the ideas and the argument to evolve and to carry implications which may extend far beyond the confines of this particular work.

What renders your dissertation unique is the subtle combination of generating with fabricating.

A music therapist embarks on an MA thesis on Interactive Rhythm. Her skill in generating (she was, by nature, a generator rather than a fabricator) was a central reason why she ran a successful clinical practice. She was severely stretched when it came to describing in words precisely what she did, to setting up hypotheses, to structuring her thesis so that it had a flow, (a beginning, middle, and end) and to completing it by the required deadline. Six months after being awarded her MA, she was able to reassess the purpose of the exercise, and was favourably surprised at how much the enforced imposition of fabricating on generating had enlarged her viewpoint.

CHAPTER III

Methodology (1)
The Spectrum of Research Approaches

1. *Where would you define your position on the spectrum of research approaches?*

2. *What strategies are you going to adopt in applying and consolidating this position?*

3. *Are your approach and strategies appropriate to your objective?*

4. *Do you like to lay down your course with a set of prepared questions and hypotheses? Or do you prefer to shape these questions and hypotheses up as events unfold?*

5. *Do you appreciate the degree of certainty afforded by numbers and statistics? Or do you recoil from such quantitative estimations?*

6. *Are you excited by seeing your art work derived from or supported by a mathematical system such as set theory? Or do you feel dehumanized by such an association?*

7. *As a mathematically-minded researcher, what virtual reality are you inventing? What Platonic forms are you dis-covering?*

Under methodology, we describe how we propose to tackle the questions and topic we have defined. In this chapter, we consider the range of research approaches. In the next chapter, we consider research strategies and designs.

The spectrum of research approaches

To get the most out of this book, it is important to understand what is involved in the spectrum of research approaches. In a spectrum, we move from one pole to another. If the spectrum is laid out in the two dimensions of a page, that means we move horizontally across the page: from left to right or right to left.

In research approaches, this polarity between left and right applies not only to the two-dimensional figure of the spectrum on the printed page. It also applies to the right and left functions of our brain as we engage these in the conduct of research. Speaking loosely, the polarities of these right and left brain functions in the spectrum of research approaches include such distinctions as those between wisdom and knowledge, mysticism and logic, art and science, meaning and cause, qualitative and quantitative measures. These predominantly right brain functions (wisdom, mysticism, art, the intuitive search for meaning, and qualitative measures) lie towards the art end of the spectrum of research approaches, i.e. towards the A end of the spectrum in Box II, p.29. The predominantly left brain functions (knowledge, logic, science, the teasing out of definitions and causes, and quantitative mathematical measures) lie towards the maths end of the spectrum, i.e. towards the F end of the spectrum in Box II, p.29

To illustrate in a little more detail. Take just one of these distinctions: meaning and cause. In human exchanges, we are often concerned primarily with disentangling confusions, making sense of the different types of information welling up from the different layers of consciousness, finding meaning in the complex communications with which we are bombarded when we try to understand another person.

Our search for meaning can take us in a number of directions, as various people have shown when they start to analyze what meaning means (see Ogden and Richards 1946). We can find ourselves unravelling a sequence of behaviour as though we were translating a foreign tongue. Or we can find ourselves creating new meanings by combining old ones in an imaginative medium. Or we can find ourselves sifting associations, seeing what goes with what, or (if the associations take on a certain sequence) what causes what effect.

Rycroft writing about his early experiences in psychoanalysis describes the obstructions he met when he tried to apply an approach based on conventional (left-brain) scientific principles, and the re-formulations he undertook as a result. These re-formulations meant accepting that different data may require different approaches at different times, and since many human happenings only occur once, shifting conditions and meaning are closely associated. In such a flux, the control inherent in formal empirical hypothesis testing, the clearcut separation of causes and effects, cannot be established. Indeed attempting to force such an approach may impair what may be achieved by a more appropriate approach using the right-brain (see further Rycroft 1985).

Conversely, many situations (the testing of a drug for example) may arise where a predominantly left-brain type of analysis is appropriate. In general, polarities in research approaches may be set up for wisdom and knowledge, mysticism and logic (e.g. Russell 1917), art and science (e.g. Holub 1990), qualitative and quantitative measures (e.g. Yin 1994).

But, an important proviso

The spectrum implies polarities, and polarities imply distinctions. We make these distinctions in order to clarify our thoughts, and as part of learning and describing a field. But the distinctions are not mutually exclusive. Wisdom does not exclude knowledge. The search for meaning does not exclude the search for causes, any more than the search for causes excludes the search for meaning. An approach through qualitative research does not exclude a quantitative approach. In all these instances, the two poles in the spectrum complement each other. In what follows, I hope you will find it helpful at the start to set up the distinctions in order to understand the lay-out of the field. Once you have obtained this over-view, you may well find you want to reach back beyond these distinctions, and discover the connections between them. It is as important in due course to dismantle the distinctions as it is to set them up in the first place. This setting up and dismantling of distinctions may reflect another aspect of the interplay between the left and right brain functions. (See further Junge and Linesch 1993. Carrithers 1992. Also Cornwell and Lindisfarne 1994.)

With this proviso in mind, here is the spectrum of research approaches. The letters A to F indicate the sections in this chapter where the particular research approach is described in greater detail. A for the section on art work will be found on pages 31–33; B for the section on heuristic research on pages 34–37; C on phenomenology on pages 37–41; D on hermeneutics on pages 42–47; E on experimental design on pages 47–54; and F on maths work on pages 55–57.

Box II: The spectrum of research approaches					
(A)	(B)	(C)	(D)	(E)	(F)
The activity					
Discovering the particular	Describing the experience of the discovery	Dissecting the discovery	Interpreting the discovery	Developing the discovery through hypothesis testing and model building	Discovering the abstract
The research approach					
Art work	Heuristics	Phenomenology	Hermeneutics	Experimental design and simulation	Maths work

EXAMPLE: MIRRORING
Mirror images in music
dance, painting etc
(art work).

What effect the experience of
mirroring has on the researcher
or the client (heuristic).

What is mirroring *per se?*
(phenomenological).

Mirroring in interpretation
eg the interpretation as
mirroring back what the patient
brings (hermeneutic).

How we measure the act of
mirroring and its effects
(experimental design).
How its use and effects
fit into models of
therapy (simulation).

Inverse transformations
and other mathematical
mirroring models (maths work).

Finding your place at any time on this spectrum of research-approaches will depend on:

1. The nature of the material being researched. Is it, for example, something relatively stable and controllable like a chemical or physical reaction? Or is it something volatile, and evanescent like a human exchange or a dream?

2. The personal characteristics of the researcher.

3. The phases in the growth of a research project. These phases may entail moves across the spectrum or moves in depth under any one heading. To understand more about such moves, we must first examine each heading in the spectrum in greater detail.

A. Art work

Do you think that a dance, a piece of music, a fictional story, a poem, a play, a painting, a sculpture, should in itself constitute research? If not, why not?
According to the definition of research given on p.1 art work would fall within the research domain. The artist certainly searches for an object, in this case a particular form through which to convey and arouse an experience. Without stretching the term unduly, artists may be said to engage in structured enquiries.

The underlying patterns of artistic imaginings inform our work even when it assumes a scientific mode. Max Planck emphasized the need for a 'vivid', 'intuitive', 'imagination' in the mind of the scientific pioneer 'groping' for new ideas, since such ideas were 'not generated by deduction but by an artistically creative imagination' (Planck in his *Autobiography*, quoted in Happold 1970, p.28. Cf Bridgeman 1950). A movement therapist senses the evolving shape of a session; a drama therapist gives a poetic interpretation. These basic responses in the arts therapist's repertoire are an inextricable part of the work and of any research arising out of the work.

This said, however, there remain some profound differences between art work and conventional research. Some of these differences will be spelt out here; others will emerge when we consider issues such as validity and reliability.

In an art work, the focus is on the unique concrete expression which may also epitomize the abstract through layers of meaning including ambiguities. 'The artist, if he deigns to notice facts at all, is likely to notice them in all their particularity' (Russell 1949, p.59). Artists court ambiguity. Their emphasis on the particular and the ambiguous introduces a new and discrepant note into the setting of conventional research which is concerned with excluding ambiguity. That is the *first* cleavage between art work and conventional research.

As artists, through the medium, we relate to the non-human environment (Cf Searles 1960), the paints, the stone, the sounds. Above all, we relate to the imaginative product, the work, which takes over and determines our decisions. The work is the reality. We relate to this non-human work with all the sensitivity that we relate to another human. Our images become separate and objectively present entities with which we can interact (McNiff 1993). Our relation to the images is both bonded and detached. How do they act on us as viewers? How do they contribute to the vitality of our world? How do they support and guide? Faust embraced Goethe every bit as warmly as Goethe embraced Faust.

We merge with our own creation as we merge with a dream. Through this mergence, we find our personal creative authority. In the twentieth century, the focus of art work is firmly centred on a personal statement...my work...which, however, has to predict or resonate a public note.

In our respect for the entity of the image, the fiction, we accept that biases inevitably distort any record written at the time or subsequently: the differences between spoken and written word; the influence of selectivity in perception, memory, mood (see further Higgins 1993, p.27 and Chapter IX). We may emphasize a bias rather than attempt to exclude it. When we create as artists, we press the point further. We purposely detach the fiction from what are conventionally read as facts. Truth comes to lie in the product and not in any immediate connection between the product and the events out of which the images in the product arise. We do not ask: did an event actually happen like this? But: can we believe it happened this way? Can we be moved by it, whether it actually happened or not? In a word, does the product 'work'?

Yin (1994) distinguishes between case-study as research and case-study as a teaching instrument. In the one, we present as accurate a record as we can muster, given all the biases we have noted. In the other, our primary concern is to illustrate a point and facts may be purposely slanted to serve this purpose. In a dissertation, we may draw on both approaches, the one proviso being that we state clearly the rules we are following. In an art work, we are committed to the latter approach. Hence the *second* break with conventional research. For to test a fiction for its relation to what actually happened is to miss the point of the fiction.

Artists usually offer their work and let it speak for itself. As creators they see no reason to explain it, though of course they may be prepared to change it. Explanations belong to critics, scholars, later generations. Sometimes the work carries the stamp of pedagogy: striking examples would be Bach's Art of Fugue, where a masterpiece evolves out of a practical illustration of a musical form; Chopin's Studies; Bartok's Microcosmos. Sometimes the focus is on exploration: Beethoven's piano sonatas or Debussy's Preludes. Often there is no ulterior motive. In somewhat the same way, in the arts therapies, the product often requires no explanation; it stands on its own.

On other occasions, an artist may offer some accompanying analysis or explanation, either in the medium of the work itself or in a different medium such as words. Examples here would be Messiaen's *Treatise on My Musical Language* as a structural support for his musical communications. Or TS Eliot's explanatory notes on *The Waste Land.*

Landy describes aesthetic research where the researchers 'document and/or analyze their creative processes while engaged in creating an art work for therapeutic purposes' (Landy 1993). Such analysis may take the form of talking with or about visual or sound images in an attempt to render them more accessible, more shareable with others.

Without some such accompaniment, conventional researchers argue, important moves may be lost. Such researchers want to know what the artist was about. What was he or she trying to do? How were they trying to do it? They want to test, take measures, check for falsifiability, replicate. Indeed these checks form the basis of hypothesis testing. In art work, any attempt to replicate another's work is apt to call forth accusations of plagiarism. Here we come on the *third* point at which art work and conventional research divide.

Artists welcome informed critiques of their work, but resent what they see as tampering with, or distorting their original communication by excessive attempts to understand it, especially if this involves them in explanatory translations in words. They experience such an exercise as an enforced sharing, like a premature or superfluous interpretation in therapy. If their product isn't potent enough to stand on its own, they are prepared to look at the product again but not so keen to analyse for others their motives in producing it.

EXERCISE SIX

> How would you evaluate the effect of art work (a painting, sculpture, concert, dance) in hospitals? (see p.106)

B,C,D. Heuristic, phenomenological, and hermeneutic research

These three approaches to research are related. In heuristic research, the activity is primarily introspection. The focus is on personal (especially the researcher's) experience, particularly as regards discovery, the excitement and burden of discovery. Examples would be studies of loneliness, or the 'inner child'.

In phenomenological research, the activity is primarily observation and exploration. The focus includes inner and outer events and their interconnection. Examples would be a study of the weather, of style in a painting or piece of music, of a segment of behaviour, of different types of mandala, of structures in the human psyche.

In hermeneutic research, the activity is primarily interpretation. The focus is on a dialogue with a person or a 'text'. Examples would be interpretations of someone's behaviour, or of a mandala as a universal phenomenon that bridges East and West, ancient and modern, conscious and unconscious (Clarke 1994, p.136).

EXAMPLE

A dance movement therapist works with an autistic child. In a heuristic study, she examines the effects of the relation on herself. In a phenomenological study, she explores the concept of autism. What is it? How has it evolved?

In a hermeneutic study, she examines her interpretation of her relation with the child, and her attempts to communicate her interpretations to the child, or relatives.

B. Heuristic research

Questions

1. *Are you particularly interested in mapping your own experience? In clarifying and articulating your own thoughts and feelings? In tracing and making sense of the patterns in your own life?*

2. *In your work with patients, are you repeatedly struck by the correspondence you find between your own experience and that of your patient? Do you repeatedly draw on this correspondence for mutual learning and expansion? Is this correspondence an important reason for any therapeutic change?*

3. *Will your dissertation be based primarily on a case-study? If so, will the focus be on the transformations that come about in the patient and yourself through the discovery of correspondences, the sharing of same-and-different experiences?*

4. *Do you use a creative medium primarily for exploring and expressing your feelings and experiences? Is your thesis to do with exploring these medium expressions, these outward projections of your inner states?*

The word 'heuristic' comes from the Greek 'heuriskein' meaning 'to find, find out, discover, devise, invent, procure'. When used in research (see, for example, Moustakas 1990) the emphasis is on the discoverer, on the reflexive experience of discovery, and the growth in self-awareness and self-knowledge that comes about in the act of any discovery. In therapy, the discoverer may be therapist or patient. (See, for example, Chapter 13 in Lewith and Aldridge 1993 on the keeping and use of health diaries by patients.) For other usages of 'heuristic' in cybernetics or to characterize models or working hypotheses, see Bullock, Stallybrass and Trombley 1988, p.382.

> A psychotherapist working with a group of bereaved parents explores the task of staying with a painful situation, of extending her threshold of pain. Instead of running away from painful memories, she stuck with them, wrote them down, drew them, re-lived them. The more clearly she could visualize them, the more she could remember, and the more the fear and pain associated with the memories were exorcized.

This emphasis on the subjective, as we saw with art work, restricts attempts to validate and replicate along conventional scientific lines. But along the lines of mergence and e-mergence, the subjective frequently grows through dialogue with another; correspondences, perceived as objective correlates, are established. Reaching inside the object, we obtain an 'inverted perspective' (Salk 1983).

> In her work with a five-year-old's school phobia, an art therapist was both exhilarated and scared by how closely the child's experience followed her own when she was the same age. As with her patient, her parents separated three months before she started her first full day at school. As with her patient, she had felt torn apart by the separation, blackmailed by both parents into 'being a good girl', loving one and rejecting the other. Thirty years on, and with the aid of her own paintings and diary, the therapist could re-live, and contain her own experiences. The pain of this reliving became the core of the support she could offer her patient. She called her dissertation: *Second time round.*

> For the theory at the back of it, she drew on two myths already developed in the therapeutic literature: the return of the hero (Eliade 1974) and the double death of Euridice (Savitz 1990).

Another set of dialogues, encouraged by the heuristic approach, grow out of active imagination where we hold on to an image that emerges in the course of a session and, then and there, or subsequently, converse and tussle with it, follow pointers however unexpected. We may act alone or with an other (see further Hillman 1983; Johnson 1991).

> As soon as Sarah left her counsellor that Friday, both knew there was unfinished business. She went away for the weekend and thought little more about it. He returned to her dream which was about not being able to escape from a deserted stockyard. He resurrected the images one by one, and interrogated them: the car that was running out of petrol as she couldn't find the exit; the one-way traffic signs that directed her round and round; the ghosts of animals slaughtered in the stalls. He began to capture the claustrophobia and the guilt. Were these the reasons for resisting escape?

What often emerges from this imaginative dialogue, this inverted perspective, is the dis-covery of what one knew but had forgotten or had never articulated, the myth we know and never know we know. Such was the intuitive awakening in a dance movement therapist in the following description:

> I had worked for weeks with Barbara and had nothing to show for it. The girl remained as shut in on herself as on the day we first met. I was fed up...with her, myself, the world, and was on the point of stopping the sessions, when something extraordinary happened. As though in a vision (I know that sounds over the top but it's the only way I can put it) I caught a glimpse of her mood. It was one of utter dejection, and though I was groping towards it as we do when the lights fuse, I was moving with an assurance like the time I suddenly learnt to swim. Picking up this mood in her lifted years of resisting it in myself. I alighted on feelings of dejection in myself that must have been around but that I didn't want to know about. With that vision, two things happened which were important to her and me: the sessions took on a new quality; I began to trust my intuitions.

Moustakas (1990) lists six phases of heuristic research:

1. Initial engagement out of which emerges the central question.

2. Immersion in which the researcher 'lives' this question, at conscious and unconscious levels.

3. Incubation in which intuition operates silently below the surface.

4. Illumination, the break-through, the vision, the turning-point.

5. Explication.

6. Creative synthesis, the depiction in an expressive medium of what has occurred.

C. Phenomenological research

1. *What do you mean by a phenomenon?*

2. *What particular phenomena have you been engaged with over the years?*

3. *Do one or more of these phenomena occupy the background or foreground of your thesis?*

4. *What are the boundaries of the phenomenon/phenomena you describe? Can you encompass the whole phenomenon or for practical reasons, will you have to carve out a selected area? If so, what are you leaving out?*

Phenomenology is the study, the science, of phenomena. The word 'phenomenon', with its plural 'phenomena', is derived from the past participle of the Greek passive verb 'phainomai', and carries the following meanings: that which appears to the senses, comes to light, comes to sight, is perceived, or observed; that which appears to the mind, comes to being, a fact, or an occurrence, the cause of which is in question; that which appears to be so and may manifestly be so or may prove to be a deception along the lines: 'things are seldom what they seem'.

Embedded in these meanings, are a number of distinctions that have taxed philosophers down the centuries:

1. Between the senses (perception) and the mind (cognition, intellection). Cf. between the physical and the mental (Berrios 1989).

2. Between appearance and reality.

3. Between subject and object.

In Western European thought, the term 'phenomena' in the seventeenth century was used to denote physical facts, such as chemical phenomena, or geological phenomena. But with the work of Kant in the eighteenth century, the term came to mean what we could grasp with our mind and was distinguished from 'noumena', the things-in-themselves, which we could neither directly observe or know, objects of purely intellectual intuition devoid of all phenomenal attributes (see further Kraupl Taylor 1967).

By the early nineteenth century, two terms were coined to designate different approaches to phenomena:

(1) **Phenomenalism**, to denote a philosophical system whereby thinkers such as Hume, Mill, and Russell re-fashioned the distinctions we've already noted between senses and the mind, appearance and reality, and between subject and obect. In particular, these thinkers were taken up with issues to do with our use of sense-data as a source for our knowledge, i.e. as a part of epistemology (see further Hospers 1967. Also Bullock *et al.* 1988).

(2) **Phenomenology**, to denote a method by which thinkers such as Hegel and Hamilton studied conscious mental manifestions. Hamilton separated the phenomenology of the mind (i.e. where we observe the various phenomena that the mind reveals) from psychology (i.e. where we investigate objectively the background, the causes, of these mental phenomena).

By the latter end of the nineteenth century, a further twist to the term 'phenomena' was imparted by Brentano when he separated 'act-phenomena' i.e. such processes as seeing, hearing, desiring, willing, from 'object-' or 'content-phenomena' which joined with 'act-phenomena' to result in conscious observation, intention, memory etc.

Husserl, one of Brentano's pupils, systematized these ideas further in what he called 'the science of phenomenology'. Coming at the end of the Cartesian tradition (which involved the root assumption that subjects know objects), Husserl argued that a subject thinks, feels, has beliefs about an object; that his or her mind is directed towards an object; and that the one thing we can affirm with certainty, is the aboutness and the directedness of this experience. Husserl called this aboutness and directedness 'intentionality', and suggested that 'intentionality' should be the basis for phenomenology, which was thus, at least in the early phases of his system, a detailed description of 'act-' and 'object-phenomena'.

It was this 'descriptive phenomenology' that Karl Jaspers introduced into psychiatry (Jaspers 1913) where he addresses such themes as the mind–body relationship, the role of scientific enquiry, subject and object dichotomy, and the criteria which enable us to evaluate the pathological in the phenomenological experience, for example by the degree to which the experience is unusual or painful to the experiencer. Above all, Jaspers distinguished understanding in which phenomenology plays a key role, from explanation, which was more appropriate to biology and genetics. He appreciated that this relation between descriptive phenomenology and biology provided an example of the paradoxical relation between the whole and particular aspects of the whole, a non-mathematical example of Godel's theorem which proved the impossibility of ever deriving a complete 'whole' mathematical system from the sum of its parts (see further in Kraupl Taylor 1967 and Shepherd 1982. For Godel, see Hofstadter 1979, p.17).

Heidegger following on from Husserl paid special attention to the distinctions between subject and object. He argued that if we look at many of our activities, we don't find conscious subjects directed towards independent objects at all. When we hammer a nail into a wall, for example, provided we are reasonably adroit, we swiftly cease to think in terms of subject and object, but operate in a 'transparent coping' mode with 'ready to hands'. Heidegger and after him Ricoeur urged that in phenomenology, we reach beyond the subject–object distinction (what Ricoeur calls Husserl's idealism). They thus opened a path to the existentialists and yet another slant on phenomena and phenomenology (see further Berrios 1989; Magee 1987).

What we should carry away from this short historical survey is, first, how varied has been the usage of the terms 'phenomena' and 'phenomenology'. In any debate, it is always important to establish which of these many uses (if any) is being employed. Second, when we engage in phenomenological research nowadays, we pursue a course along the following lines:

> a systematic analysis of the contents of conscious awareness including material objects, immaterial 'systems' such as music and maths, and our experiences of thoughts, pains, emotions and memories.

an analysis of what something is and not what causes it. In phenomenology we let things show themselves as they are in themselves (Magee 1987, p.257).

an open-minded enquiry into whatever area we direct our search, with a ruthless dissection of the assumptions we meet in ourselves and the field. Comparative anthropological viewpoints may assist us in testing our deepest assumptions (see, for example, Lewith and Aldridge 1993, Chapter 16).

EXAMPLES

A group of counsellors studied the phenomenon of a crisis. One focussed on what crisis meant to different people who suffered it, how they defined their personal 'crisis'. Another looked at what crisis meant to the different people who intervened and sought to care for those in crisis. What led them into this work? A third considered how a crisis can provide the opportunity for personal growth, for more effective coping, both in victims and carers. Crisis can be a 'breaking of habit'. A fourth examined phases in the course of a crisis again as these affect victims and carers. What sort of measures are demanded at any particular phase? A fifth planned her project on crises at different times of life. A sixth directed his search into crises resulting from unemployment. A seventh scanned the roles of different members in a team operating to relieve crisis victims with particular attention to who fulfils the role of advocate for the patient (cf Wright 1993).

An art therapist, who practised transcendental meditation, became interested in 'falling through the gap between thoughts into an object-less trance-like state'. In his thesis, he examines what is necessary to achieve this state (the focus of attention, repetition of events like chanting a mantra) and the difficulties standing in the way of reaching it. He contrasted this meditational mode of being with his practice of art therapy which he saw as more to do with the evocation of images than with their erasure. He considered the possibility of moving between these contrasted experiences of 'emptying' and 'filling'.

A social worker examines the early stages in the phenomenon of 'burn-out' across a number of subjects including herself.

Phenomenological studies frequently reach deep into the frame of a topic. Examples of phenomenological psychology would be studies on forms of spatiality, the lived moment, remembering, awakeness (see further Straus 1966 or Jaspers 1913). The frame may surround an individual, for example the phenomenology of a hallucination, or it may surround a group, for example the dynamics and myths in groups of different sizes; the shifting roles of a consultant in a large group (Turquet 1974, 1975).

In open-ended interviews, a music therapist examines his own and fellow therapists' experience of improvization. What are the key phenomena in that experience? His dissertation moved into action research when he extended his search to include the experience of colleagues improvising in drama, dance, and art therapy. His aim was to construct a 'shared language' in the experience of improvization (cf Forinash 1993).

A similar exploration was carried out by another music therapist into experiences having to do with the 'moment of hope' in 'guided imagery'. What phenomena linked music with transpersonal imagery evoked in patient and therapist? (cf Kasayka 1991).

Three dance movement therapists explore in separate though related · dissertations a patient's experience of a stroke, Parkinsonism, and residual paralysis in polio. What does it feel like to have to cope with a stroke, a tremor, widespread paralysis? Through mirroring these effects in themselves, the therapists explored the phenomenology of coping styles.

A psychiatric nurse attached to an ante-natal clinic works in depth with four mothers, comparing how they feel towards their child when it is still in the womb with how they feel towards it, hold and relate to it, for three weeks after it is born. She develops her dissertation as a comparative phenomenological study about: Changes in attitudes that go with giving birth.

D. Hermeneutic research

1. *Are you particularly taken by the idea of entering into a dialogue with another person or with a text, a manuscript, a picture, a piece of music, something someone else has made?*

2. *Do you enjoy relating to a product from another era, or another country? Do you enjoy transposing this historical or geographical journey into your own time and place?*

3. *Does this dialogue include interpreting what the other means? When do you voice this interpretation? When do you keep it to yourself?*

4. *Can you listen to other people and respect their otherness, whilst at the same time being aware of your own situation, your own point of view, your prejudices?*

The word 'hermeneutics' comes from the Greek 'hermeneuein' meaning 'to interpret a foreign tongue, to explain, or expound'. 'Hermeneuein' in turn was derived from the name *Hermes*, the messenger of the gods. Hermeneutic research then entails the interpretation of 'foreign tongues', God's messages, a 'text' which may be a human artifact such as a child's story or drawing, a piece of music, a video of a dance. Or the 'text' may be another human (or non-human) whom we address in a conversation (see further Bullock *et al.* 1988; Ricoeur 1981).

Just as phenomenology grows out of heuristics (understanding oneself is one side of understanding any phenomenon), hermeneutics grows out of phenomenology. For a similar circular pattern exists between understanding and interpreting. Since interpretations are tentative explanations, hermeneutics may be seen as an early bridge across the descriptive/explanatory divide defined by Jaspers (1913) (see also p.39).

> A music therapist asks what a patient is trying to say in a particular passage of improvisation in the same way as he might pose the question in his interpretation of a text by Bach.

> An art therapist listens to a patient's comments on a drawing the patient did last week. While the therapist listens, her interpretation of what the drawing meant – made to herself at the time when the patient did the drawing – is slowly modified.

A counsellor seeks to make sense of eight-year-old Sally's apparently 'crazy' behaviour in the face of a disaster. He begins to formulate an interpretation that would satisfy such questions as: what did the disaster mean to the child? What did certain aspects of it symbolize for Sally? How did these aspects link with past and present events in her life? How can I convey, the counsellor asks himself, through my interpretation that I understand what she is suffering?

In the dialogue that develops between interpreter and interpreted, each has their separate historical and cultural context. Historical context implies a tradition, with a 'fore-structure', a set of preshaping expectations and assumptions (prejudices and stereotypes). Thus the basic pattern of any hermeneutic exchange is:

Interpreted

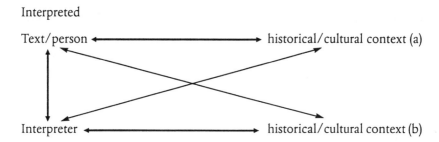

Text/person ⟷ historical/cultural context (a)

Interpreter ⟷ historical/cultural context (b)

Because of the different contexts, there is an inevitable distance between interpreter and interpreted.

An art therapist finds he can't abide certain periods of art history. These periods lie outside his own time and country. In forcing himself to examine what he called 'his resistance', he said something snapped. He felt dragged out of the enclave in which he'd spent most of his life. 'My horizons were stretched'. What before were stereotypes took on new meaning.

Language itself can be treacherous. We should never assume that two people are using the same word in the same language in the same way. Even the same word used by the same person in a different context can take on an opposite meaning. A 'good catch' can have a warm feel when used in a cricket, fishing, or marriage bureau context. The 'catch about that situation', i.e. the snag about it, conveys a quite different feel. In ironic exchanges such inversions are made purposefully. ('I had a smashing time.') Problems of translation are well recognized by anyone who's tried to translate a poem from one language into another. A diagnostic label such as 'schizophrenia' can denote a different disease in different countries (Van Os *et al.* 1993); Bettelheim (1983) demonstrated how certain translations of key words in Freud's text can alter not just the nuance but the basic message.

In any dialogue we need to recognize this potential chasm between the two parties involved. People reading a text are themselves part of the meaning they apprehend. So the ultimate success of any dialogue will depend on the capacity of interpreters (and interpreted if a person) to open up their enclaves, catch a glimpse of themselves in their context, explore the overlap of horizons and move towards bridging the gulf between them. It depends on the capacity of the two to refrain from dogmatism, be open to but not absorbed by the other, to be both other- and self-critical, to live with a plurality of ideas, and with long periods when no one wins (see further Clarke 1994, p.144).

It is we who make the texts speak, by posing questions and interpretations to which the text provides answers. To interpret means precisely to use one's own preconceptions so that the meaning of a text or a person, as in the instance of counter-transference, can open up. Gadamer (1975) emphasizes the reciprocal relation between interpreter and text, the mutuality of understanding. It's through the text, through others, that we come to know ourselves. Hermeneutics in this sense is the complement of heuristics.

The dialogue between interpreter and interpreted may move in an inward direction to involve a dialectical discussion between conscious and unconscious along the lines of the familiar diagram:

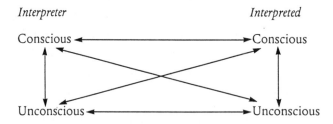

As part of this inward direction, any dialogue may involve multiple levels of actual and phantasied figures:

In a dissertation along hermeneutic lines, a counsellor talks with a child in an attempt to understand the child's feelings about his parent's divorce. In this dialogue, the counsellor mapped out the following levels:

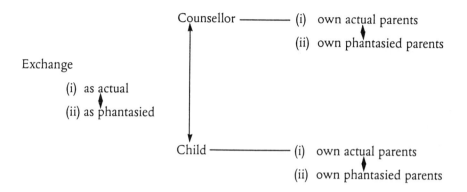

The dialogue may move in an outward direction to involve the larger world of symbols and beliefs. Jung looked to revivify twentieth century consciousness through a dialogue with myths and traditions of past ages. He believed that in a dialogue with the past, we may discover new ideas, and save the present from ossification. Historical comparison is not a mere learned hobby, but a practical and useful exercise which sometimes opens doors that had seemed inexorably closed (Jung CW18, p.1269).

> A movement therapist was struck by the way Rameau recycled the spiritual essence of the various dance forms (gavotte, minuet etc) into his operas and then back again into his keyboard pieces. She became interested in the way the spirit of the dance symbolized many aspects of French life at this time. Her first dialogue was with French musical texts in the eighteenth century. Here she was assisted by several useful studies on the music and the dances of the time. Her second exercise was to update this dialogue into her own experience of the dance in twentieth century Paris. Like an archaeologist, she found herself considering residues and possible equivalents.

We may develop a symbol, itself an analogy, through an ever widening network of metaphors and analogies. Jung called this process amplification, and it plays an important part in any hermeneutic study (see Ricoeur 1978 on the rule of metaphor), both to grasp the meaning of a term and as part of a quest for underlying psychological identity. Examples include amplification of a dream image in a poem or painting; amplification of memories and meanings in a story; amplification of a musical motiv or a movement (e.g. Chodorow 1991; Bartal and Ne'eman 1993); amplification of a symptom in relation to an archetypal image.

An offshoot of the dialogue is the so-called hermeneutical circle, the interplay between the movement of tradition and the movement of inter-preter, another version of the whole/part distinction we met in Jaspers' thought (see p.39). Here the distinction refers to how the deeper meanings of a part have to be discovered from the context, i.e. ultimately from the whole (Gadamer 1975, p.167).

Interpretations involve a hierarchy of meanings, both in an individual and even more in a group.

> In a hermeneutic study of a family, a counsellor described how, in a family group session, different members began to draw portraits of each other, describe each other, and interpret these pictures and descriptions. The counsellor in turn interpreted these interpretations to the group.

We need to be aware of the limits of any interpretation. One such limit concerns the hermeneutic model itself where the binary distinction between interpreter and interpreted inevitably inclines the outcome of any debate towards a similar binary form such as 'West is extroverted, and East intro-verted'. Such distinctions can become simplistic and question-begging (see further Clarke 1994).

We have already touched on problems inherent in the act of interpretation: the gap between interpreter and interpreted, arising in part from their separate contexts. Paradoxically, these problems may be compounded (through lack of definition) or eased (through a 'common language') when interpretations are made in a non-verbal medium. In a musical or dancing group, a dialogue often occurs with a speed of interchange that is immediately slowed down and distorted by any interpreter who attempts to translate from the non-ver-bal to the verbal medium. Something similar may occur in a clumsy or premature interpretation in psychotherapy.

What is at issue here is the complex relation between interpreter and interpreted. Through an interpretation, therapists can easily influence their patients into coming round to their, the therapists', viewpoint. How do we get into someone else's shoes to reach an interpretation yet leave room for that someone else (be it patient or audience) to find their own interpretation? Winnicott reminded us that psychotherapy is not the doling out of clever interpretations but the giving back to the patient what he or she brings to us (Winnicott 1972, p.137). How does the interpreter overcome an inevitable tendency to appropriate the other?

The converse of this situation may also hold and bring a different set of problems. As good interpreters, constantly adapting to the interpreted, we may find that far from appropriating the other, we are granting validity to a number of apparently contradictory opinions. No interpretation is timelessly true, correct in itself, completed (another version of Godel's theorem). So how come any one view may be read as 'superior' to another? How can we distinguish well-grounded from unsound positions? If everything is relative and changing, on what basis can we judge one interpretation to be better than another? Or for that matter, how can we retain our own identity?

EXERCISE SEVEN

How do you measure a good interpretation? (For some suggestions, see p.106).

E. Experimental design and model building

What do you see as the value and the limitations in building up knowledge through the hierarchy of hypotheses, theories, and laws?

For Tim Lancaster, *Clinical Epidemiology* by Sackett, Heynes, Guyatt and Tugwell was a book that changed his medical practice. Based on the McMaster medical school belief in an evidence based approach to clinical problems, the book drew on biostatics, epdemiology, probability theory, and decision analysis, to judge the meaning of clinical data, and to sift diagnostic and therapeutic strategies. It provided Lancaster with 'a framework for communicating clinical judgements in a way that can be exposed and analysed' (Lancaster 1993).

Setting up, estimating, and testing hypotheses

At the back of most researchers' minds lurks a hypothesis. Where their projects differ is in how clearly this hypothesis is articulated. In improvisational studies, Bruscia (1987, p.525) distinguishes between those that advocate from the start detailed planning with specific goals (hypotheses) and those where the planning and goals emerge in due course. In the debate between positivism and naturalism, the issue similarly is at what point in the procedure do we set up hypotheses, and with what clarity. The point at issue is not over whether or not we can dispense with hypotheses altogether. We can't (see further Hammersley and Atkinson 1983).

Formal, empirical, experimental research is based on the idea of building and testing hypotheses according to the principles of induction and deduction. The situation may be summarised in the following diagram:

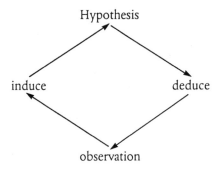

laws of evidence   laws of logic

probability   valid argument

empirical truth   analytical truth

A hypothesis may be established with or without the aid of quantitative measures. An interpretation in psychotherapy may be read as a temporary hypothesis, which is tested by what happens afterwards between patient and therapist, by, that is, the effectiveness of the interpretation (Hinshelwood 1991. See also Exercise Seven p.47). Miller's (1993, p.252) action research in institutional settings contains many examples of hypotheses being set up and tested without resort to quantification and statistical analyses.

'The part played by measurement and quantity in science is very great, but is...sometimes over-estimated' (Russell 1949, p.67). Russell points out that science is not co-terminous with quantification. A law may be 'quite scientific without being quantitative'. There are times when we must be content with these qualitative laws that are 'none the less scientific for not being quantitative'. The contrast between qualitative and quantitative approaches does not necessarily mean that one is more logical (scientific) than the other (Yin 1994, p.14. See also Forinash 1993).

Usually in the formal experimental approach, quantification is introduced to muster statistical support for assessing the probability that a hypothesis is true or false. We shall return to this when we consider analytic tools in Chapter VI (see pp.78–94).

Variables

As the word suggests, a variable is any measure that varies from person to person or object to object, or in the same person or object, over a number of trials. Height is a variable. So is body weight or hair colour. Different people have different heights, weights, and hair colour at any one time. So in recording these differences you would be recording three variables. A person has different heights at different stages of growth. So you might record changes in this one variable over a period of time.

A variable is any event that can be defined and measured in some way. The fluctuation of abnormal movements in a case of Parkinson's disease might constitute a variable, as might location of lesions in the nervous system.

A counsellor wanted to investigate the reasons for bouts of bizarre behaviour in an adolescent client. She listed as variables:

(a) some of the possible causes for the behaviour such as loss of job, loss of boyfriend, a recent miscarriage, drugs

(b) some of the features of the behaviour itself such as outbursts of rage, periods of confusion, withdrawal, headaches.

A movement therapist wanted to test what effect, if any, a course of therapy sessions was having on a patient's development. She listed as variables:

(a) certain features of the therapy that might have some effect such as the exercise, the enlargement of movement repertoire, the enthusiasm of the therapist, the support of a group, the excitement of the music.

(b) certain features that might change in her patient such as lifting of depression, improved self-esteem, more aware social responses, lowered blood-pressure, enhanced muscle-tone.

Both these examples have to do with sifting causes and effects. Such sifting of cause and effect underlies much experimental research. The set of variables marked (a) in the two examples may roughly be considered as possible causes, and the set of variables marked (b) as possible effects. In experiments, the set of variables marked (a) would be termed independent; the set marked (b), dependent since we register their response to the independent variables.

In experiments, we have then:

Independent variables	Dependent variables
Causes	Effects
Interventions	Outcomes. Responses to interventions

If we think that a course of arts therapy sessions has some effect on a person's development, our independent variable would be the course of arts therapy, and our dependent variable some measure of its effects, such as improvement of self-esteem, lowering of blood-pressure, enhanced muscle-tone, changes in social responses amd so forth. These measures of the dependent variable will be calibrated on various scales such as rating-scores for self-esteem or social response, a chart for blood-pressure, a graph for muscle-tone.

Hypothesis

A hypothesis is a statement postulating a relation between two or more variables. We might, for example, attempt to tie together in a hypothesis an independent and a dependent variable. In a patient with Parkinson's disease we might hypothesize that

Variable A (independent)	Variable B (dependent)
Certain parts of the nervous system are damaged	Certain abnormal movements occur

The centrepiece of experimental research is the hypothesis, the statement to confirm which is the object of the research. If we think one variable may have an effect on another, then we carry out an experiment to see whether it does have such an effect. We call the variable that might exert the effect the independent variable, and we call the variable that registers the effect the dependent variable.

A third type of variable called a hidden or confounding variable is the variable accidentally overlooked when the experiment was set up. Subsequently in the course of the experiment, the hidden variable is found to be exerting an influence on the results. This influence is separate from but overlaps and may outweigh any influence exerted by our independent variable. A hidden variable thus confounds our results. It is the *first* reason why our experiment may be invalid. That is, the results we arrive at do not accurately represent the aim we claimed to be testing in our hypothesis (see further in Davey-Smith and Phillips 1992).

In a hypothesis, we now have the situation:

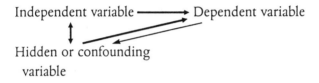

This hidden or confounding variable may be the play of chance. Much of our efforts in an experiment are devoted to excluding chance. So in contrast to our hypothesis, we set up the *null hypothesis*, namely a statement postulating that any relation we think we have established in our hypothesis could have come about by chance. If the null hypothesis is correct, our hypothesis would then be falsified and not proven. Our experiment is designed to disprove the null hypothesis.

Population and sample

A population is a set or collection of objects (including people) in which the variable occurs. The student body is a population as are patients in arts therapy or patients with Parkinson's disease. We might be interested in exploring the effects of an arts therapy (the independent variable again) on a group of old people, or housewives, or accountants, or priests, or toddlers, or married couples, or psychotherapists. Any one of these different collections represents our selected population. In isolating one of these groups in this fashion, we define the population on which we intend to focus our attention.

This definition of a population will appear in our hypothesis, in our null hypothesis, and in our results, and will set clear limits on the problem we are addressing. If our conclusions wander inadvertently beyond these limits, this will be a *second* source for invalidating our results. For example, we may inappropriately extend our findings to a much larger group than the one we have defined. This criticism has been levelled at attempts to generalize from Freud's limited population of middle-class, late nineteenth century Viennese.

The position is rendered more precarious by the need to *sample* whatever population we define. A sample is a selected subset of a population (for example, a representative group of patients with Parkinson's disease). It is rarely feasible to include every member of a population we decide to study, even though we have limited that population to a particular group. We could hardly go around testing every clergyman or toddler in the county of Middlesex, let alone the UK or Europe. So we have to settle for a selected sample that obeys certain strict rules. It must accurately represent the population being sampled (representativeness); it must be large enough to satisfy statistical criteria (size). (For further details on representativeness and size see p.82.) Clearly, if our sample is biased in some way, any conclusions we draw from it will be influenced by this bias. We cannot be sure that statements made about a biased sample will hold for the population from which the sample was drawn. If we can not be sure that the population on which we have based our conclusions accurately reflects the population as defined in our hypothesis, our experiment becomes invalid. Sampling errors are a *third* source for invalidating experiments.

A population can consist of one person since in any one of us a multitude of collections (populations) are available for testing.

In a hypothesis then the researcher postulates some association between two or more variables: a course of dance movement therapy sessions (independent variable) enhances muscle tone (dependent variable); painting a nightmare (independent variable) reduces the level of anxiety aroused by it (dependent variable); group-drumming (independent variable) increases sociability (dependent variable).

In a null hypothesis, the researcher postulates that any such association between two or more variables could have come about by chance. The aim of any experimental research is to test the null hypothesis, i.e. to prove or fail to prove that it is false. If the likelihood of the null hypothesis being true can be shown to be remote (a chance of, say, one in a hundred) then we may assume the null hypothesis to be false and if that is so, we may accept our hypothesis as valid until a better attempt at dislodging it can be mounted. What experimental research gives us is a body of ideas that stand as yet unrefuted on the grounds of probability. That is the nearest we can get in science to proving them true. We estimate the likelihood of an event or set of events being false. Our aim is to show that a certain set of events is most unlikely to have occurred by chance.

EXERCISE EIGHT

> How would you go about establishing whether homeopathy is effective or not? What are some of the problems you might meet on the way? (For some suggestions see p.106)

Theories, models and laws

A theory or model is what we construct to enable us to derive, explain, and predict one or more laws. We build it out of one or more (temporarily) proven hypotheses. In a model we set out, often in formal mathematical terms, the lessons believed to have been learnt from experience, and thus expose to all who can read, the bases on which we form our judgements. Through a good model, we can correctly predict what our hypotheses are suggesting.

Examples of theories and models: different types of theories in the social sciences (Yin 1994, pp.28–30); Miller's societal model analogous to an economic model (Miller 1993, p.271); the links betweem movement, emotion, and the striato-cortico-limbic system suggesting the infra-structure of a possible psycho-neurological model (Joseph and Young 1992, especially Chapters 47 and 49. Also Higgins 1994). For particularly lucid instances of applied mathematical models see the Open University programmes on mathematics.

> In exploring the foundations of multimedia arts therapy, an art therapy student and a music therapy student plan a joint dissertation on synaesthesia (i.e. the capacity to fuse perceptual channels, to experience auditory events as visual or tactile ones, to visualize tastes and smells and so on). The two students were especially interested in the theoretical model that neurologists were evolving to explain synaesthesia. In outline this model suggested two possible connections in the brain:

cortical ⟵——————⟶ cortical connections

limbic connections

The students designed their research with a view to testing the validity of these two connections in the model.

In the experimental approach, we aim at discovering a natural law out of one or more proven models. *A Law (of nature)* is regarded as an empirical proposition possessing: a universal regularity (or invariance); a hypothetical form (If..., then...); an infinite range in space–time; a potential for predictions; a relation to a larger system of laws into which it fits with a greater degree of generality. (*Example:* the law of gravity). Like any other humanly devised law, it may hold for a time before being replaced. For the purposes of this book, the idea of a natural law is best thought of as an ideal to know about and aim towards, but not one that need detain us further at this stage.

To summarize. In the experimental approach:

1. Defined variables determine the hypothesis and a series of hypotheses define a theory or model, which may progress to a law of nature such as gravity:

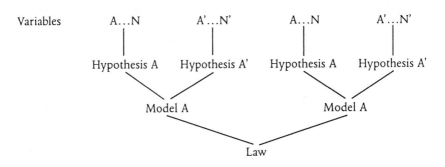

2. Defined variables are measured in a population which has to be representative and large enough to satisfy statistical criteria.

3. A hypothesis must be testable and so falsifiable (Popper 1934).

4. Testing a hypothesis on quantitative grounds is based on disproving the null hypothesis.

5. (Temporarily) established hypotheses, and theories or models to which they lead, are confirmed or modified by the degree of their predictive success.

F. Maths work

Can maths work on its own constitute research? If not, why not?

In maths work, we focus on developing a logical system with increasing degrees of abstraction. The system determines its own shape just as the novelist finds his characters determining the shape of his novel.

The abstraction works in two ways. By honing down, cutting out irrelevances, we reach the core of a concept. The definition of a line for example, as that which joins two points, cuts out all other aspects of lines we meet in everyday life.

Second, by detaching concepts from their physical context, we can increase the generalizability of our observations. Our honed down definitions leave large physical areas in our concepts undefined; we can transfer our chain of reasoning the more easily from one context to another.

Being contained within the laws of logic, the critical criteria for maths work are more precise than are those for art work. Hence in the climate of the twentieth century, the marriage of maths work to research is more acceptable than the marriage of art work to research. We enter this marriage of research with maths work through the circle of pure and applied maths. In theory, we draw out, in pure maths, our logical systems without reference to the physical world at all. In applied maths, we develop our systems in conjunction with observations derived from the physical world. In practice, as maths withdraws 'increasingly into the upper regions of ever greater extremes of abstract thought', it returns back to earth 'with a corresponding growth of importance for the analysis of concrete fact... The utmost abstractions are the true weapons with which to contend our thoughts of concrete fact'. (Whitehead in Kline 1953, p.519. Cf Wilder 1978.)

In the marriage of maths work and research, the mathematical model *first* may underpin our findings.

> A group of music and dance therapy students got together because they wanted to know more about certain mathematical models they sensed lay at the back of their work. They parcelled out their dissertations according to the different ways they related to these models. Two students, one in music and one in dance, were interested in notation, and started to map out systems of notating in their chosen medium in terms of set theory. The musician drew on set-theoretical analyses of atonal music; the dancer drew on mathematically based semiotic studies in choreography. Three other students, two in dance and one

in music, began to apply geometrical concepts of space to their improvisations. One of the dancers worked on the kinesphere, i.e. the shapes in which we move in space, and which are analogous to the Platonic solids (cubes, tetrahedra, etc). The other dancer pursued an analogy she discovered between country dance forms and the structure of mathematical groups. The musician began to investigate the links between pitch, temperament, and vectors in space. Two further students, again one a dancer and the other a musician, started to look at the mathematics underlying rhythms, which they found were playing an increasingly significant role in their work.

Second, maths work may function as a predictive system divorced from the senses. It may conjure up vistas that we cannot see with the 'phenomenal' eye (Russell 1912). For example, in non-Euclidean geometry, mathematicians deliberately went against conventional experience to explore areas that would never have been conceived had we relied only on sense experience. Through maths and technology, we can now explore the most unexpected musical structures.

The limitations of maths have been well rehearsed, not least by mathematicians themselves: its basis in rationality (see Kline 1953, p.526); the human limitations on the capacity for abstract thought; the cultural and intuitive bases, which are subject to the shifts and vagaries in the evolution of cultural intuitions (Wilder 1978, p.200); the unrepeatability of much human experience; synchronicity (Clarke 1994, p.63); the incompleteness of any mathematical system (Godel's theorem. Also Russell's paradox. See Magee 1987, pp.306–7); the insubstantial basis of many deep-rooted mathematical concepts (Begley 1992).

Russell defined maths as 'the subject in which we never know what we're talking about nor whether what we're saying is true' (Russell 1917, p.75).

One final point: the link between art work and maths work. The artist focuses on the unique, the concrete individual instance. Maths is concerned with the abstract, the general law. Yet through the unique, the artist arrives at the general (see for example abstract art and the idea of music as the most abstract of the arts). Similarly, through the abstract, the mathematician arrives at the concrete.

In the spectrum of research approaches, we have come full circle. A close affinity between their different approaches is often experienced among artists and mathematicians (see for example the works of Xenakis and Stockhausen.

Also Holub 1990, especially his essay on poetry and science). The joining of the circle is one final example of the complementarity of poles in the spectrum, and of right and left brain functions.

CHAPTER IV

Methodology (2)
Research Strategies and Designs

1. *How do you plan to translate your chosen research approach into a practical strategy and design?*

2. *Will you be exploring, describing, or explaining? Or all three?*

3. *How clearly will you be able to articulate your hypothesis?*

4. *How much certainty (rigour) will you hope to introduce into your strategy design?*

5. *How much time and experience do you have available for the degree of rigour you propose?*

Research strategies and designs are the means we use to apply and consolidate our basic research approach. These means will serve different aims and conditions. Here are some different types of research strategy design.

A. A case report

This is a description of an unusual or exemplary case. From your case work, you will already be familiar with some of the headings and structure which need to be borne in mind when you write up a case for your dissertation (See further Higgins 1993). The most detailed case reports will be found in the depth psychology literature, for example the *Journal of Psychoanalysis*, or the *Journal of Analytical Psychology*. Case reports that reveal such intimacies may pose problems of confidentiality; certainly the question of clearing the position with the patient, and the question of what effect this is likely to have on the treatment, will need careful consideration.

These precautions would also hold for a detailed case study in action research or in the socio-anthropological field.

The wide choice of what events have been recorded, what have been selected from the record, and how these selected scenes are presented, links the case report to research approaches that lie towards the art work end of the spectrum of research approaches. When, partly for confidential reasons, the case report verges on fiction, the links with art work may be particularly apparent. The case study becomes a roman à clef: a romance where story and characters become a key to a real life situation.

B. A single case (n=1) experimental study

Here the essential model is one we have already met in section E in the previous chapter.

Before   After

Intervention

The Baseline   New Baseline

In a series of randomized trials the patient acts as his or her own control (as in a within group design) and the results can be submitted to univariate or multivariate analyses.

For example, the design may follow a serial variation: AB, ABA, or ABAB, where A represents the measures taken during the baseline (the period when the independent variable, for example the arts therapy, is *not* operating) and B represents the measures taken during the phase of intervention (the period when the independent variable *is* operating).

These measures may be found to follow a normal distribution. In this case, we compare the distribution during the baseline A (the control set of scores) and the distribution during the phase of intervention B (the test set of scores). We examine the difference between the means of the two distributions and calculate the likelihood of this difference between A and B being significant (see pp.85–88).

Alternatively, we can search for correlations between events happening during A, or between events happening during B, or between events happening in A as compared with events happening in B (see Higgins 1993, pp.92–5).

We can also watch the passage of events in A and B for changes of slope and changes of level. We can apply methods of analysis derived from studies on similar patterns of movement (time-series) such as the fluctuations in regularly recorded economic indices (see further in Lewith and Aldridge 1993 Chapter 12; Kazdin 1982; March *et al.* 1994 along with a follow-up letter from Saunders 1994 linking N=1 trials with a standard randomized, double blind, trial).

The advantage of single case research is its closeness to clinical practice. The primary purpose of the research is to measure the treatment benefit for the individual along lines that can be tailor-made for this particular person. The research encourages the co-operation between therapist and patient, who can become a co-worker in the research and assist in decisions over flexibility of approach, and variation in levels of rigour. (Cf the patient who is prepared to keep a diary of events in the treatment and to share this diary with the researcher. See further Chapter 13 in Lewith and Aldridge 1993.) The research provides a direct measure of an individual's (as distinct from a group's) change. These individual varations are now recognized as an important component in our response to illness and treatment (Lewith and Aldridge 1993, p.118). Single case studies are thus important both as measures of this variation and as a basis for co-operative research among therapists comparing these individual differences through systematic replication. Single case research also avoids major difficulties, such as recruitment of large numbers, and the cost and administrative management of clinical trials.

Single case research may play a significant role in assessing events where cultural differences in beliefs and attitudes figure prominently (see for example suggested research strategies for assessing the effectiveness of herbal remedies in Lewith and Aldridge 1993, p.398).

The disadvantages of this type of research lie in the limitations imposed on the nature of measurements. One needs to be sure of a stable baseline out of which arise clear-cut changes. These changes should be reversible (back to baseline) and without prolonged carry-over effects. Singlecase research is

·not particularly appropriate for acute or labile problems. A second limitation concerns the nature of controls, particularly the lack of any between-group type of control.

Generalizations in singlecase research can only be built up through systematic replication, since each piece of research can only refer to the particular case under scrutiny. But this pattern of generalization applies to caselore in general and is a further instance of the closeness between single case research and clinical practice.

C. A case series

In many preliminary dissertations, a favourite design is where we draw on several cases to illustrate some particular phenomenon such as a peculiar movement or posture, a particular mode of improvising, or a diagnostic category (autism, depression). The cases may be cited as vignettes, certain aspects being selected to illustrate certain points. Often the series represents a section of our caseload: patients for example whom we know have undergone a particular type of treatment.

A case series, like a case report, is often the earliest occasion when we begin to have a hunch, that leads to a hypothesis. Through a case series, we often engage in a pilot study. By using the cases as instances to explore and exemplify a more general issue, we may feel less constrained to record rigidly precise details that might jeopardise a subject's right to anonymity.

The main limitation of a case series is that it may lack the rigour of more formal clinical trials.

D. A cohort study

A cohort study is a particular type of case series. In it we define and observe a group of people who have a specified characteristic, and who are followed up over a period of time with a view to detecting changes in this characteristic. The group might be those who regularly attend a youth club for a particular reason; or certain musicians who regularly meet for an improvisatory session; or patients with a particular diagnosis who have undergone a particular treatment.

The changes we observe give to a cohort study the quality of a film, a moving image, growing and developing over time. In this type of study, we also take a step closer to distinguishing between those who have and those who have not a certain condition. Among the 'have nots' we begin to define our controls. (See further under G).

E. A survey

If we think of a cohort study as equivalent to a film, a survey or cross-sectional study, is like a still, a snapshot, taken at a particular point in the sequence. In it we aim to estimate the presence and frequency of certain patterns: for example the prevalence of 'depression' or 'obsessionality' in a selected group of people.

An infinite number of patterns are available for survey. As we select them, we may quickly find we are setting up hierarchical structures, a series of sets within sets. Out of those people suffering from 'depression' (subset A), we may go on to look, for example, at patterns of behaviour among these 'depressives' (subsets of subset A), and even at patterns within these patterns (subsets of subsets of subset A). Alternatively we might start by isolating a certain behavioural response eg smoking in our sample (subset B) and go on to see how many smokers were 'depressed' (subset of subset B) and of a particular age-group (subset of subset of subset B). Any of you who have conducted a library search on a computer will recognise similarities with these hierarchical survey systems and indeed there are close links between surveys, classifications, and bibliographical searches. A point to which we will return when considering the literature review (see pp.69–77).

In a survey, as with the cohort, we need to define clearly our selected groups, the population we wish to survey. In an extended, formal, survey, we need to ensure that the sample we go on to select from this population is free from selection bias, truly representative, and large enough (see further on randomization, minimization, stratification, statistical power p.82).

The core of the survey is the questionnaire where the guiding principle is to distil what we want to find out into the minimal number of questions, each shorn of all ambiguities. A good guide on how to design a questionnaire for a survey may be found in Stone (1993).

If all the appropriate precautionary measures have been taken, the answers to the survey questions (the raw data) may be quantified into various scales (see pp.85–86), transposed into comparable measures such as percentages, and analysed with the aid of descriptive and inferential statistics (see pp.85–89).

A formal full scale survey is thus one of the more elaborate hypothesis-testing techniques. It should only be undertaken when we have a relatively clear idea of what we want to know, and what hypothesis we want to test. An informal survey, in which we sift possible comparative patterns, and examine possible hypotheses, may be undertaken at any time, and serve as a link between a case report, a cohort study, and more rigorous extended designs such as a formal survey or a clinical trial.

F. An archival or historical search and analysis

A topic is chosen such as the history of a certain style, group, or movement in music, painting, or drama. In choosing such an archival or historical search and analysis, you may find yourself stitching together a hermeneutic approach (contrasting the historical context of the topic with that of yourself) with survey designs of greater or lesser formality, and cohort designs investigating changes over time. The whole exercise will bear many resemblances to the literature review (see Chapter V).

G. A case-control study

Just as the cohort study grows out of a case series, the case control study in turn grows out of the cohort study where we started to compare the 'haves' with the 'have-nots' (the controls).

In a case control study, the comparison becomes the focus of attention being formalised into observations on those with a particular condition (eg some illness) and observations on a selected group without this condition (the controls).

We might for example set up a more formal study comparing painting or movement observations in a group of patients with Parkinson's disease with painting and movement observations in a group without Parkinson's disease.

A key feature about any such comparison would be the attempt to make the two groups (experimental and control) as like as possible apart from the one feature that we are seeking to measure namely the presence or absence of the disease. We would try to 'match' the two groups for age, gender, social status etc. and so minimize the influence of variables that might distort or confound the influence of the disease.

H. A controlled trial

A controlled trial is an experimental study in which one group is exposed to an intervention, and the outcome is compared with that in a similar group who have not been so exposed. For example, a group of patients are given a particular drug (the intervention) and the outcome is compared with that in a group who are given a placebo (ie an innocuous medicament made up in a form that is indistinguishable from the experimental drug).

The essential feature of the clinical trial is the rigour we exert in our attempts to exclude confounding variables. As in a case control study, we ensure the two groups are similar by careful matching or by such techniques as 'within-patient' designs where advantage is taken of matched sites such as eyes, or ears, for testing the independent variable (eg eye drops in one eye against control placebo of sterile water in the other) or 'cross over' designs where the same patient receives both treatments (the independent variable and the control) one after the other, the order being decided randomly. (See further Lewith and Aldridge 1994, p.12.)

We exclude the potential biases of selection by randomization; we exclude the potential biases that arise from knowing whether we give a drug or a placebo by 'double-blinding' (in which neither receiver or giver knows in any instance whether placebo or drug is administered. See further Lewith and Aldridge 1993, p.35); we exclude the biases of past observations by undertaking the whole exercise prospectively.

Some further available choices

From this brief resumé of research strategy designs, it is clear that we have a number of further choices. First, we can choose whether to use the strategy design to explore, describe, or explain a set of events. The further up the scale we move from A to H, the more we shift from exploration to explanation (see further Yin 1994, pp.3–4).

Secondly, in each of these strategy designs, we adopt a particular attitude towards time. There is a polarity between a case report, or an archival search, where by definition we are looking backwards, retrospectively, and a controlled trial where we examine the different outcomes prospectively (see further Fowler and Fulton 1991, and Doll 1992). In between these two poles, we can choose to run our case series, cohort, and case control studies, prospectively or retrospectively. In a survey, whether formal or informal, we map the state of things as they exist in the present.

A third choice that is open to us in all the strategy designs except the case report is over the degree of rigour we decide to impose. A distinction is conventionally drawn up between *observational* studies where researchers simply observe what is happening and *experimental* studies where they seek to control the conditions under which their observations are made. But there is a range of mixtures between these two types of study. Even in a case series, we can introduce a technique such as randomization if the numbers are large enough. The more of such techniques introduced, coupled with the setting up of the study prospectively rather than retrospectively, the more we approach the experimental gold standard of the randomized double-blind prospective controlled trial. For this reason, a single case (N=1) study, or a case control study, can on occasion be indistinguishable from a controlled trial (Saunders 1994).

A dilemma in research strategy-design

The choice over degrees of rigour in research design raises a dilemma that everyone engaged in research should know about even if they are not personally involved. We touched on one aspect of this dilemma when considering the price one may pay in obeying the dictates of a statistically correct experimental approach (see pp. 18–19). Here the problem may be seen to be broader based.

To start with a salutary reminder:

> Despite there being some 30,000 biomedical journals in the world, only about 15% of medical interventions are supported by solid scientific evidence. This is partly because only 1% of articles in medical journals are scientifically sound, and partly because many medical treatments are not assessed at all. (Eddy, as reported in Smith 1991. Cf also Andersen 1990 who reckoned that less than 28% of papers from the top-flight medical journals were free from some design flaw.)

No one would dispute that this is a highly unsatisfactory position, demanding more critical scepticism and more rigorous checks. One snag however is that the more insistent our demands for rigour, the greater the likelihood of running into major problems in the experimental design. The challenges and hazards that face anyone undertaking full-scale adequately controlled trials such as the gold standard of randomized, double-blind prospective design are now well-recognized (Kramer and Shapiro 1987. Herxheimer 1991, 1995. Sykes 1994). The hazards include funding, especially in countries where research budgets are tight (Garner *et al.* 1994. Also Rous 1994); recruitment, including ethical and political issues over the rights of patients and minority groups (see further Brandon 1991, Warden 1991, Lewith and Aldridge 1993, p.96 and p.124); management of people once recruited, for example how to cope with those unwilling to take the placebo because they don't want to miss out on the drug or those unwilling to take the drug because of its unknown effects (see further Macbeth 1994 and Pollock 1993). Small wonder perhaps that a recent review of such randomized controlled trials warned that conclusions were often faulty because of some basic errors in design and analysis (Nowak 1994).

Are there approaches that entail less rigour and hassle, and that we can run in parallel with the gold-standard controlled trial? Two lines have been suggested. The first stems from observational or outcome studies (e.g. Orchard 1994). Here the controversy is about how we are to interpret data derived from studies that, on the one hand, represent a 'disciplined systematic aggregation of collective clinical experience' (see Delamothe 1994, Greene and Maklan 1994) yet, on the other hand, may be inadequately controlled (Sheldon 1994). Brennan and Croft asked if we can justifiably use measures of probability significance, for example, in studies that do not include randomization in the selection of cases (Brennan and Croft 1994)? Their paper drew a robust response (Slattery 1994). Comparisons were made with economic models where sophisticated moves are used to detect the confounding variables that might arise in the absence of randomization (Buck and Sutton 1994). What is required, in other words, may be more not less statistical analysis: in particular, a more explicit statement of the implicit models being used so that the assumptions can stand revealed (MacManus 1994). This way, practice can begin to be based on sound knowledge of which interventions cause what difference (Delamothe 1994. Also Lewith and Aldridge 1993, p.115.)

The second line that is increasingly being used to bolster the information from controlled trials, without actually undertaking new ones, is what has come to be known as meta-analysis: the collection, amalgamation, and re-analysis (using the latest statistical techniques) of a selected number of past trials. In the controversy sparked off by this new arrival, the protagonists are evenly divided over how feasible it is to assume that meta-analysis itself can attain adequate standards of rigour (see further Chalmers and Haynes 1994, Clarke and Stewart 1994, Cookson 1994, Dickersin *et al.* 1994, Doll 1992,

Eysenck 1994, Groves 1994, Thompson 1994, Tognoni *et al.* 1994). The effect of chance on the outcome of clinical trials and systematic reviews of trials seems to be much greater than many investigators realise (Counsell, Clarke and Slattery 1994).

The dilemma over the 'gold standard' and alternatives poses further problems when we enter the field of medical anthropology and confront different definitions and ways of exploring such issues as holism, measurement and truth (see further Lewith and Aldridge 1993 pp.96, 99, 191 and chapter 16).

EXERCISE NINE

> A psychotherapist writes a case-report on a patient whose wife divorced him after 14 years of marriage. The patient came into therapy in a state of depression two months before the decree absolute and developed a colonic cancer eight months later. The therapist had read an article in her local paper saying that cancer could be caused by divorce. Enumerate the questions she might ask as she sifted the evidence for the article's hypothesis (see further pp.106–7).

To summarize, depending on time and resources available, the research strategies and designs open to you include:

Box III: some research strategy designs

A case report: an extended description of an unusual or exemplary case.

A single case (N=1) experimental study: follows the principles of the formal experimental approach, using the single case as its own control.

A case series: several cases, cited as vignettes, to illustrate a particular phenomenon, which may be heuristic, hermeneutic, or the basis of an evolving hypothesis.

A cohort study: a population who show a specified characteristic, and who are followed up over a period of time with a view to observing changes in this characteristic.

A survey: a population is surveyed for the presence and frequency of certain patterns. An archival or historical search and analysis: some analogies with the literature review.

A case control study: a comparison of two groups: the 'haves' (test) and the 'have-nots' (control).

A controlled trial: a more rigorously designed comparison of two groups where one is exposed to an intervention and the outcome is measured against that of a similar group who have not been so exposed. The design includes randomization, double-blinding, and prospective search: the so-called 'gold standard'.

CHAPTER V

The Literature Review

1. *Have you honed down your questions so that your topic now has clear boundaries around and within it?*

2. *Have you planned the boundaries of your study precisely enough to avoid being thrown by known restraints of time and resources?*

3. *How does other people's work bear on these boundaries?*

4. *How clearly defined are the boundaries in the relevant work of other people?*

5. *Have you covered the relevant field or at least a representative sample?*

6. *Have you included references that run counter to your own opinions?*

7. *How impartial have you been towards other's work?*

8. *How thorough has been your assessment of the relevant texts?*

In the literature review we:

(i) find out what has been discovered about our topics and related fields and so set further boundaries on our topics.

(ii) carry out a meta-analytical survey of others' findings, conclusions, and viewpoints.

Once we have defined our topic and methodology with some precision, we are ready to look at what others have done in our chosen field or in fields related to it, and to ask how effectively they have done it. The sequence may not be as clearcut as the last sentence might suggest, depending in part on our personality. Some like to sort out their own ideas before attempting to take in other people's. Others prefer to have some inkling of what's going on elsewhere before they set out on their own course. Others, perhaps the majority, choose to run the two exercises together, sifting their own questions and topics in the light of what they discover from fellow workers.

This may well be your own experience in the course of writing your dissertation. For though the brunt of the literature review may fall within a section entitled as such, we often find it cropping up again in the methodology section, in the discussion section of our findings, and in the conclusions when we are considering further steps.

Some dissertations may consist solely of a literature review: others that are breaking new ground may only have a few paragraphs about the literature, since few or no papers have been found in it. The nature of a literature review in studies that lie to the art work end of the research approaches spectrum will differ from a review which lies towards the maths work end and which will be more concerned with issues of empirical research design, such as sample size and statistical measures.

(i) The literature review as a means for setting boundaries

In defining the topic of our thesis, we engage in splitting off what we are going to cover, the units of analysis, from the Other that we are not going to cover. This process of definition spreads to include not just the title of the topic but the various ideas, concepts, and experiences we will be selecting in the course of it. Sometimes the topic may lead directly into an established system such as the family, or the human body. We may then, for practical reasons of limited time and resources, or for more general reasons to do with the form and coherence of our project, be faced with the problem of deciding which parts of the system have to be selected, and which parts excluded. A critical examination of the literature can often give us some guidelines on such decisions.

> A child psychotherapist, in the first session with her twelve-year-old patient, found herself facing a series of sexual issues that clearly involved the whole family. Later she wanted to include these experiences in her thesis on Adolescent Sexual Identity. Her reading of the literature alerted her to several ethical issues about permission and confidentiality, and to the major difficulties over disentangling whose role was contributing what influence to the patient's identity. As a result, in part, of her excursions into the literature, she was able

to decide how far she should go in describing the sexual experiences of other family members as these emerged in her own and colleagues' interviews.

Terry's infantile eczema went on to asthma, attacks of which in due course triggered off bouts of migraine, which in turn resulted in problems over food allergies, and keeping regular hours at work. When writing up the case for his thesis on Absenteeism, Terry's counsellor was guided by an extensive literature review in deciding how to define focus and boundaries in the potential tangle of dermatological, respiratory, neurological, alimentary, and socio-psychological sub-systems.

A counsellor becomes interested in the sort of behaviour that characterises 'depressed' clients. A quick survey of the literature revealed how easily she might be snared if she followed the elusive term 'depression' through sadness, withdrawal, retardation, disinterest, manic defences etc. She settled instead for using a validated rating scale.

A dance therapist was struck by the different emotions that different movements elicited in a group. He found a short critical review of the literature invaluable in assisting him to by-pass the philosophical conundrums of the body–mind problem.

This issue of *setting boundaries* deeply affects our work. When we embark on an exercise such as a thesis, it's only natural (and right) that we should be full of high hopes and enthusiasm. These are apt to spill into our ideas on what we can cover in the time available. Aims swell out of all proportion to what realistically we can achieve. The shadow side of this over-ambition is to underestimate the significance of the corner we have carved out for ourselves.

These over or underestimates of our work's status are also likely to determine the attitude we take up towards others who have worked in the same field. On the one hand, they may be denied any credit for getting there before us; on the other, they may be idealized, revered, their every utterance presented as a gospel-truth, beyond the reach of any criticism. In either event, this over or undervaluation of our work may mean our writing is hindered by an unnecessary sense of awe…either at what we have set ourselves, or at what others have already encompassed. If we can again subliminally remember that whatever exercise on which we embark is a finite phase in our research career, we may be able to keep things in proportion, and so lighten our load.

EXERCISE TEN

> Start to talk in your imagination to the writers whose papers you have selected for review. Humanize these names you have put in brackets with a date after them, or listed in a lengthy impersonal bibliography. Have them sit down beside you and tell you about how they came to write the paper, the context of their work, the questions they were asking, what they wanted to know and why. Humour them.

Our capacity to define may determine both our choice of topic and the way we proceed with it. With training, we can often sharpen our intuitive sense for ideas that can be sculpted by definition. Under these circumstances, the more we can hone down what is relevant from what is not, the more precise and telling the questions we may be able to ask. Pasteur observed that chance favours the prepared mind. A cool critical review of the literature provides repeated occasions for such a preparation.

(ii) The literature review as a meta-analytical survey

We have met the idea of survey and meta-analysis in Chapter IV when we were looking briefly at research strategies and designs. Here we meet them again with the same basic meanings but without any necessary quantitative associations.

What we survey in the literature review is the collection, the population, of texts we have drawn from our sources. Given the pressures of time, we may only be able to sample a part of this collection, but, as in a survey, we will need to pay close attention to the nature of this sample: what questions are we going to put to it, what answers do we (expect to) receive from it, and what conclusions do we draw from these answers.

To get the most out of this particular survey, we must see how meta-analysis comes into the picture. In research developments arising out of extended clinical trials, what was meant by the term 'meta-analysis' was the pooling of information from a set of selected (experimental) studies. Our literature review is a form of meta-analysis in that we process information along similar lines (though without any reference to quantitative measures). In it, we carry out analyses at two different levels: an analysis of our relation *to* the works we are reviewing; and an analysis of the relations *within* these works themselves.

Consider for a moment an analogy with the supervision that many of you may have experienced in the course of your case work. Your supervisors may have to attend at any one moment to a number of levels: their relation to their supervisee; the supervisee's relation to the patient; what's going on in the patient's world in and outside the treatment sessions; other patients or events that come to mind and that may be relevant to the discussion.

In scanning the literature, you, as reviewer/supervisor, need to attend to a similar set of levels:

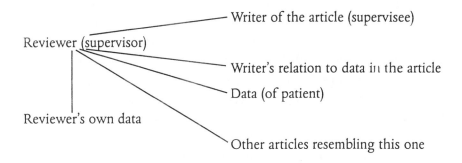

Writer of the article (supervisee)

Reviewer (supervisor)

Writer's relation to data in the article

Data (of patient)

Reviewer's own data

Other articles resembling this one

The levels of the meta-analytical survey

The sources on which you draw include:

(a) **discussion** with anyone who has already researched this or related fields. These discussions often turn up the most immediate and relevant texts. They have the great advantage that you can assess at first hand the results and the quality of selection (and selector) in the literature that you are scanning.

(b) **informal talk with colleagues and friends.** Once your mind is focussed on a topic, it is surprising how often chance items find their way to your attention from most unexpected sources. From informal talks, through associations, new avenues open up, along with new or forgotten usages of words, and other ways of looking at your findings.

(c) **reliable textbooks and journals** in accessible libraries. Your main source, it is subject to the familiar limitations implicit in any publication: the writer's and publisher's selectivity and bias.

(d) **CD/ROM computer searches**, (for examples of bibliographical databases see Lewith and Aldrige 1993, p.445–8) and

(e) **Internet, e-mail, if you have access to a modem.** Major snag in both sources d) and e) is the hidden selectivity of journals, abstracters, and translators. What is elusive is any assured and consistent quality, editing, and hierarchical organization in the overload of information (see further McGrath 1994).

In sifting the literature which backs up your topic, you should aim at an exhaustive search. But given the time limits under which you have to work, this aim may become more of an ideal than a reality. You may have to abandon any attempt to cover the whole field and settle instead for examining in detail a selected number of references (a representative sample).

The aim is to identify key texts, that is texts that are central to your topic, that contain the most relevant references, that report the most relevant work with the most trustworthy conclusions (as distinct from speculations or research with serious methodological flaws). These key texts represent the respondents in your survey sample.

In our meta-analytical literacy survey, the points we need to watch have **first** to do with **information sources**:

Have we properly identified our sources and is the sample we have selected representative?

> A music therapist wants to explore the effect of music on various heart conditions. He combs the literature for all relevant studies. He has an uneasy feeling that his sample may not adequately cover the field of possibilities. He discovers why when he catches himself dismissing a study where the findings clearly contradict his assumption that his therapy has a beneficial effect. He realizes there may be many more such studies that have not been published for the same reason. People don't want to know about conflicting evidence. He concludes that his literary survey sample as it stands cannot be representative if there has been this (unconscious) urge to distort the evidence. He emphasizes this point early on in his literature review.

What were the criteria we used in selecting different elements in our sample? Were these criteria adequate guard against the bias of selectivity? What would be the effect of changing these criteria of selection?

Second, we need to watch the flow of **questions and answers**. In any survey, a crucial point is how umabiguous and free from slant are the questions that are asked. Are these unambiguous questions drawing unambiguous answers?

In a meta-analytical survey, the situations may be represented diagramatically as follows:

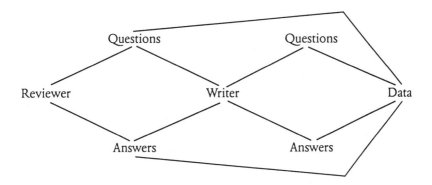

In our survey-sample, how clearly focused are the questions the writers put to their data? Where and how do these questions touch on our work? In turn how well focused are our questions to their work? What answers did the writers receive from their data? What answers did we receive in turn? Did the questions asked in our review and in the articles reviewed net the range of answers they were designed to catch?

> An art therapy student was working on a dissertation about visual imagery in states of depression. She had amassed an extensive literature but as soon as she began to sift it, she realised that, because the term 'depression' was usually left so vague in the papers under review, the questions the writers were asking spilled out in all directions, left little in common between themselves, and posed major problems for her when she tried to articulate them with the questions she was asking herself. The result of her brief review was a return to logic and phenomenology, and the drafting of an operational definition of depression on which she could then re-start her topic.

Third, we need to watch our **analysis of these answers and the conclusions we draw from this analysis**. (Points touched on here are taken up further in Chapters VI and VII.)

In a survey, we analyze the answers we obtain from our population-sample according to the rules of evidence, backed up where feasible by statistical tests for degrees of probability. In our literature review, we develop information from our sources along the same type of analysis. Are the findings in our review, and the findings in the articles reviewed, valid? (For different types of validity see pp.83–85)

Can we be sure we are not slanting the information from our readings in directions we would like it to go? Have we excluded as far a possible the various types of bias in our analysis? (For different types of bias see pp.32, 52, 64). Are we observing appropriate rules of deduction and induction? Did the writers of the articles we are reviewing follow the same principles?

> A counsellor reviewing some literature on drug taking began to suspect that strong moral convictions in several of the writers might be slanting their presentation. He first checked on their bibliographies and from a quick assay found their choice of texts in line with the slant he suspected. He then looked in more detail at their experimental designs (where these were available) and began to find major discrepancies in the make up of their test and control groups. While he himself had strong views about drug taking, he had equally strong views about basing these on biased reasoning. The discrepancies he discovered in his review of the literature assisted him in his moves to eradicate similar flaws from his own experimental designs.

Are the conclusions in our review and in the articles reviewed based on evidence, rather than on belief or 'authority'? In our conclusions, have we stayed within the boundaries justified by the evidence? Did the authors of the articles reviewed do the same?

> In reviewing a paper on why art therapy had a certain physiological effect on a group of patients, a student begins to question whether the heuristic approach and case series design in the paper had gone far enough to move out of exploration–description and into explanation. The paper included some impressive figures for measuring the physiological effect but on closer scrutiny these so-called 'dependent variables' were ill-defined and uncontrolled. In addition, the numbers

involved were far too small for the ambitious statistical analysis presented. In an imaginary dialogue, the student asks the writer why he found it necessary to over-reach himself. Why not stay with description? He had included many good observation. In her dissertation, the student noted that though the conclusion might be validated at some future date, it could not be supported by the evidence as presented in this particular paper.

(See further Oxman 1994. For empirical experimental studies, Fowler and Fulton 1991 give a useful assessment checklist.)

EXERCISE ELEVEN

Construct short abstracts of the main references you have collected for your review. Check the arguments. This exercise should assist you in organising your sources and serve as a good preparation for when you come to abstract your own dissertation (see pp. 101–2).

To recapitulate:

Box IV: summary check-list for the literature review

Have you adequately identified your **sources**? Are there enough of them? Are they good enough? Are they representative? Have you checked for bias of selection?

In any **article**, have you checked the flow of questions and answers? Are you satisfied with the chains of evidence, and the validity of deductive arguments the writers have employed?

In your own **assessment**, have you checked your investigative techniques, and the validity of your conclusions?

CHAPTER VI

The Findings
Collecting, Analyzing, Presenting and Discussing

1. *How will you prepare and collect your findings, your database?*

2. *Do your findings relate to your topic? To your propositions? to your unit(s) of analysis?*

3. *How will you analyze and organize this collection?*

4. *What criteria are you adopting for demonstrating validity? Reliability?*

5. *Do you present your findings effectively?*

6. *Do your findings give body to a theoretical model?*

7. *How will you display the meaning and implications of your findings in their own right and in relation to others' work?*

In this section, we consider:

(i) our own contribution to the dissertation: our findings, or database, and how we collect, analyze, and present them.

(ii) the meaning of these findings, and how they relate to others' work, to a theoretical model, and to the context of our topic.

(i) The findings or data-base

Just as questions shape and are shaped by topics, and topics shape and are shaped by research approaches, so the nature and lay out of our findings will shape and be shaped by the overall research design. Across the range of research approaches, strategies, and designs, what we find and how we write up our findings are both subject to wide variation. In a heuristic study on a detailed case report, the findings may take the form of an uninterrupted narrative derived from diary entries, autobiographical sketches, or internal dialogues. In an experimental study on the effects of some intervention (a clinical trial), the findings will include, for a start, a precise definition of this intervention (the independent variable), along with a description of precise reliable outcome measures (the dependent variables) in the defined sample.

Your relation with your dissertation needs to remain flexible throughout, responding to developments in the way that good therapists respond to the changing demands of their patients. Whilst a run of unexpected findings is unlikely to shift the basic strategy or approach (causing you to embark on a survey for example rather than a case report), it can frequently cause you to alter the lay out of the particular strategy or approach you have selected.

> A drama therapist embarks on a phenomenological enquiry into multimedia therapies: what patients are most likely to benefit by what particular arts therapy? With colleagues, she begins by selecting patients according to their stated preference for drama. Soon after starting sessions with a group of nine, she comes on issues which she had not taken fully into account when she began. Several patients decided they wanted to change to a different medium. Should she subscribe to their request to work in a channel that previously perhaps had been suppressed? Does work in one channel imply suppression of a shadow channel? Is an important breakthrough in their therapy a switch into the suppressed channel? Can she perhaps cater for this switch by adroit use of her own medium, drama? How interchangeable are experiences in the different media? Is this an issue of synaesthesia? how able is she, the therapist, to convey visual, auditory, tactile sensations through the words and gestures of drama?

> She begins to lay out a prospective case series design in which she will follow what happens when someone changes their medium and someone doesn't, paying special attention to those who wish to change but decide not to.

A. Collecting the findings

Before starting to collect, some people like to draw up a plan of action, complete with a rough time scale, for interviews, experiments, etc. (For a comprehensive preparatory schedule see Moustakas 1990, p.48). Drawing up such a plan depends in part on the complexity of your design. A big advantage is the fillip the plan can sometimes give to reliability: anyone replicating your study can follow the details of your plan. A disadvantage can be that the plan interferes with spontaneity. (See further in Yin 1994, p.55–63).

Another preparatory move is to use an early interview as a pilot test ie one that will assist you in deciding on degrees of relevance for future questions. (See further in Yin 1994, p.74. Also Harris 1986, p.64 and Lewith and Aldridge 1993, p.16 and p.35).

The sources from which you draw your data resemble those we've already met when we considered collecting sources for the literature review. As conversations or written texts, your sources may include documentation such as your own notebooks, sketch pads, letters, memoranda; case reports, test results, patients' drawings and writings, sound and video recordings; interviews, with an individual or group, and ranging from the open-ended informal conversation to the strictly focused session with a carefully worded set of questions that all participants will be asked; experimental records, the detailed description of your design and the data that emerged when you carried it out.

In interviews and experiments, you may wish to co-opt one or more colleagues (particularly if you are using recording machines as in movement observations or musical improvisations). An additional data source may then stem from your co-worker's experience.

> A counsellor wants to investigate how people overcome an autistic streak. Where am I going to get my cases? He looks through his own list which is still quite short as he's not been in the field very long. He finds one case that is possible and indeed was one of the reasons starting him off on the idea. He talks to friends and hears about another instance not unlike his own. He finds a novel in the library which covers the same ground and gives him further pointers. Slowly a dissertation along phenomenological lines begins to come together.

Frequently we tap more than one data source.

> A movement therapist videotapes a session which includes movement sequences and discussions with the patients about these. She has access to the case records which contained detailed histories, psychological tests, patients' drawings and poems.

Drawing on these multiple sources, we have a choice of procedure. We may wish to converge these sources on to one particular issue we wish to explore, and then sift the evidence that arises about this issue as seen from these different angles, so-called triangulation from navigational methods for plotting one's position geometrically using three bearings. (See further Lewith and Aldridge 1993, p.243).

The measures the movement therapist wanted to explore in one patient concerned the prevalence of 'light movements' (as defined in the therapist's theoretical model) in the patient's movement profile. The field of enquiry the therapist set up looked like this:

Direct observation: Patient's assessment
  Her own   of his own movements
  Her co-worker's

                        light movement

Videotape analysis: Group discussion of
  Her own   findings among colleagues.
  Her co-worker's   The patient's views about
                                         the videotapes.

Alternatively, we may explore our different sources without converging them on any focus. We read our multiple data sources (documents, interviews, etc) as a set of parallel and sometimes overlapping channels.

The movement therapist might build up a picture of her patient by staying with the following main data streams:

movement sequences	therapist's reading of these	and conclusions
the patient's comments on his movements, his life, and progress.	"	"
the patient's poems	"	"
others' comments on the patient's progress	"	"

In a heuristic, phenomenological, or hermeneutic study, emphasis will be on the depth and penetration of open-ended interviews. The inter-human, I–Thou, exchange may open up 'what would otherwise remain unopened' (Buber 1965, p.86) with all that implies for researcher and researched alike. The sort of questions researchers might be addressing would be: what stands out vividly in their own and their respondent's experience? what feelings, thoughts, bodily changes, occur? what forms of expression are used: story, conversation, harangue, song? (See further Moustakas 1990.)

In an experimental study, the emphasis will be more on defining the eligibility of the (human) sources (Lewith and Aldridge 1993, p.5 and Chapter 7). Is this collection going to provide me with an appropriate sample? Am I staying within ethical guidelines in isolating and manipulating this sample, in exposing it to interventions such as certain types of questions?

An appropriate sample must be **representative** and of adequate **size**. If we are drawing on quantitative assays, it is essential to get these two features settled before starting. (See Lewith and Aldridge 1993, pp.13, 29, and 36 about the size of samples.) But for safety, seek statistical advice to avoid later disappointments.

Collecting the sample may also involve decisions about:

randomization, ie using random numbers to assist in selecting and allocating patients and events. (See further Harris 1986; Lewith and Aldridge 1993, pp.8, 22, 34.)

stratification, i.e. ensuring that the randomized groups are appropriately matched for such characteristics as age, gender, status…(Lewith and Aldridge 1993, pp.10, 23. For matching see Altman and Bland 1994f.)

minimization i.e. minimizing the difference between treatment groups in respect of prognostic variables (Wickham 1994).

obtaining **homogeneity** in a group e.g. ensuring that patients included in a clinical trial show a comparable set of symptoms.

ensuring sample **untaintedness** e.g. not using the same patients when we are testing a hypothesis as were used in generating it (Andersen 1990, p.39).

B. Analyzing the findings

Collecting and analyzing go hand in hand. Every observation we record is loaded with analytic questions: Why did I select this event or set of events? How come it happened like this and not like that? What am I missing out? How else might one view the whole scene?

In analysis, we are also concerned with an argument, or a chain of evidence. What is the connection between this event and that? Have I drawn the right inference, made the right connection? Does my argument make sense? Is it sound **(valid)**?

Sometimes, especially in experimental work, we are also concerned with **reliability** i.e. repetition, replicating someone else's study or laying down guide lines so that someone else can replicate ours. (See further Lewith and Aldridge 1993, pp.60, 131.)

VALIDITY

The word 'valid' (from the Latin 'valere' 'to be strong') carries at its core the idea of strength, soundness, and efficacy. So 'validity' implies a quality that is backed by (legal) authority, soundness, well-founded. Something with 'bottom'.

At this point, researchers diverge in their usage. For some it is the patient's or therapist's experience that needs to be validated (see, for example, Heal and Wigram 1993, p.116). For those following the formal experimental approach, it is the accuracy of the findings that needs validating and the validity of an experiment is often felt to rest in excluding the bias of patient's or therapist's convictions.

In approaches that lie to the art work end of the research spectrum on p.29, validity is measured by how accurately, vividly, comprehensively, an experience is captured and conveyed. The checking, judging, accepting, the 'constant appraisal of significance' (Bridgman 1950) are the confirmatory acts in validation, and may involve an ever widening circle from single researcher, through respondents, co-workers, to the global audience of an art work.

We validate a piece of music, a painting, a poem, by the question: 'does it work'? Other musicians, painters, poets, critics, admirers and denigrators, may agree or disagree with the judgement. Along with aestheticians, philosophers, they may dig around in the hope of discovering why it works or doesn't. Few would question the question, which includes such issues as integrity, sureness of aim, depth and resonance. Compare this attitude towards the validity of an art work with an experimental approach which seeks to validate the effect of art works in surrounds such as a hospital. (See Miles 1994 and exercise six p.33.)

In experiential research, analytic validation involves immersion in the records of the experience. In heuristic research, this experience is primarily that of the researcher; in phenomenological research, it is that of the phenomenon itself; in hermeneutic research, the experience is that of interpreting. Out of the immersion comes the identification of themes and specific atmospheres, first for each participant individually, then the slow emergence of a composite picture. (For a more detailed description of the analytic process in heuristic research, see Moustakas 1990, p.51.)

In action research, such as the exchanges between patient and therapist, or client and consultant, an important measure of validity rests with how well the presenting problem has been clarified, and modified. The task a patient or an organisation may pose us may turn out quite differently from what at first appears, and the value of clarifying a defence mechanism may lie in the light it throws on the larger system rather than on any immediate need to dismantle it. The constant question in validation here is whether the patient, client, or organization is functioning more effectively as a result of our intervention.

In the experimental approach, to say that the experiment is valid means that, as a result of it, we have been able to prove what we set out to prove. Further qualifications of validity refine this general meaning:

In **Face** validity we ask if a measure we have adopted is, on the face of it, a reasonable indicator of what we are asking it to measure. Is it a credible variable?

In **Construct** validity we set up appropriate operational measures for whatever concepts we are studying. Can the results be correlated with accepted gold standards? For example, in examining changes we might expect from our therapy, attention to construct validity would entail selecting specific types of change and showing that specific outcome measures do indeed reflect these defined changes. Do the components of our measure cover all aspects of the attribute they are measuring (also known as their **content** validity)?

In **Internal** validity we establish a causal as distinct from a spurious relationship. Used in explanatory studies, the goal of internal validity lies at the root of our efforts to exclude hidden and confounding variables.

Through **External** validity, we define the domain to which our findings can be generalized. We mark out the boundaries of our selected populations.

In **Predictive** validity, we ask whether a measure will predict future differences.

Pursuing **Criterion** validity, we ask if a measure can be easily replicated, and if so, are similar values obtained (cf reliability).

Validity may also be qualified as **Concurrent** or **Prospective**. (See further Yin 1994, p.33 and p.94. Lewith and Aldridge 1993, p.60.)

STATISTICO-MATHEMATICAL TECHNIQUES AS ANALYTIC TOOLS

In the formal experimental approach, with research designs such as case control studies, surveys, or controlled trials, data are usually collected on a quantitative basis. As a result we can use probability space and a variety of mathematico-statistical techniques in our analysis.

> Two student movement therapists sought to organize their findings from a small-scale survey they had carried out. One student had taken measurements of height, weight, musical skills, movement skills, literacy and numeracy quotients, from 100 subjects. This they called Data-set A. The other had taken the same measurements from 200 subjects. This they called Data-set B.

Using **descriptive statistics**, they noted first the different scales that underpinned their measures. There were three:

An **interval** scale where a defined interval (say 15 cm) is the same at any point on the scale where it's selected. (The distance between 120cm and 135cm is the same as the distance between 50cm and 65cm.) This scale underpinned their measures of height and weight.

An **ordinal** scale, where we rank our findings in order but cannot assume that a defined interval is the same throughout the scale. Ordinal scales are often used in psychological measurements, such as intelligence, where we can say that an IQ of 150 is greater than an IQ of 140. But the gap of ten points, say between an IQ of 150 and 140, is not the same as a gap of ten points between an IQ of 110 and 100. Ordinal scales underpinned their measures of music and movement skills, and literacy, numeracy quotients.

A **nominal** scale where we are dealing with categories that are either there or not there, turned on or off like an electric light. A nominal scale underpinned their measures of male and female.

For future reference, they knew that each of these scales would require a different approach. (For a good introduction to the choice of statistical approach see Greene and D'Oliveira 1989). But for the moment, their next step was to **transform** their immediate measures (their raw data) into percentages so that they could compare some aspects (such as the proportion of males and females) of Data-set A whose subjects numbered 100 (N=100) with a corresponding aspect of Data-set B whose subjects numbered 200 (N=200). The percentages were close enough for them to decide there was no major difference between their samples for these particular aspects.

Returning to their raw data, they then took measures of **centrality and spread**. With data on their interval scales, height and weight, they plotted a certain type of frequency distribution. That is, they plotted the measures obtained from their scale (heights from 120cm to 180cm) against the number of people in their two populations achieving a particular score: how many were 120cm, how many 135cm, how many 150cm and so on. The resulting pattern of frequency distribution, as they expected, began to take on the shape of a bell, the so-called normal distribution.

From this type of distribution they obtained two key measures. The first was the measure of centrality: the height of the bell, the greatest number of people recorded for one particular height, or weight. This particular measure is known as the mean or average.

It is calculated by dividing the sum of the scores by the number in the sample. The second key measure was one of spread from this average peak. Moving symmetrically down the curve on either side of the bell from the peak, this measure of spread is given as so many 'standard deviations' from the mean. A standard deviation is arrived at by another simple formula connecting numbers in the sample with their variance from the mean. A further measure of spread, the standard error, is closely related to the standard deviation, and is used in comparisons of means. (For further details see Swinscow 1990, Hayslett and Murphy 1979.)

For data measured on their ordinal scales, they used the median instead of the mean, and what are known as non-parametric statistics to obtain measures of centrality and spread. For organizing data measured on a nominal scale, they used different non-parametric statistics such as the chi-squared test.

These principles of **descriptive** statistics may be summarised as follows:

Scale Interval	Normal distribution with mean and standard deviations	Parametric statistics
Ordinal	Skewed distribution. Median used as measure of centrality	Non-parametric statistics
Nominal	Tabular distribution	Chi-squared test

The two movement therapy students then wanted to examine in greater detail the relations between various data sets: eg between Data sets A and B; and between sets within a combined Data-set A + B. Were there any connections between heights and weights? male weights and female weights? weights and movement skills? weights, movement skills, and literacy quotients?

Here they needed to draw on **Inferential statistics** that are designed to answer two basic questions. The first: what is the **degree of probability** for any difference we note between selected sets (eg the difference between mean heights or mean weights) being due to chance? How often are we likely to meet such a difference in our sample: once in ten comparisons? once in a hundred? once in a thousand? The standard way of writing this is p (for probability) is $\leq$ (equal or less than) 0.1 (one in ten) or 0.01 (one in a hundred) or 0.001 (one in a thousand).

The second basic question is: for a certain defined value (such as a mean), a certain defined sample size, and degree of probability, what is the **interval** within which one can **confidently** expect the variation to swing over a series of trials? Put differently, within what range of results for this size of sample can we be reasonably confident that the differences we detect are significant (at a chosen degree of probability). The standard way of writing the confidence interval is to give its upper and lower limits, or the central point +/- (plus or minus) half the interval.

(A close connection exists between confidence intervals and size of sample. The smaller your sample, the wider the confidence interval; the wider the confidence interval, the less likely are your results to carry any statistical significance. This is one of the many reasons you should consult a statistician before you start on any quantitative exercise.)

> The two movement therapy students considered how they might apply these inferential statistics to their comparison of groups for one or more variables using established research procedures such as **analysis of variance**, **correlation**, and **regression**.

Through **analysis of variance**, we can measure differences within and between the groups we isolate, determine whether such differences are likely to be brought about by chance, and assess how accurately these findings in our sample reflect those to be found in the population from which the sample was drawn.

In **correlation**, we seek an index of association between one variable and another. This index is a number which tells us whether the association is close, tenuous or non-existent. We call the index a correlation coefficient and arrive at it by using a formula which relates the variance of our two variables.

Where we are searching for the effectiveness of a test, the correlation coefficient will be one of validity. By means of it, we can determine the extent to which the test is measuring what we hoped it would measure. Where we are searching for replicability and confirmation of our test by others, the correlation coefficient will be one of reliability. (For examples of correlation patterns see Chapter VIII in Higgins 1993. Also see Altman and Bland 1994a. Persaud 1994.)

In **multiple regression analysis** we 'fit' a line which follows the direction of a correlation and which runs as closely as possible to all the points plotted. (For further details see Schroeder *et al.* 1986.) This line we call the regression line because it embodies the mathematical regression of one variable on another (in this case y on x). The regression line has certain valuable properties:

1. A starting point or intercept where it cuts the y-axis.

2. A slope, defined by a number known as the regression coefficient. The slope represents the ratio of the amount of change on the y-axis to the amount of change on the x-axis, and allows us to predict (roughly) the score on the y-axis if we know what it is on the x-axis, and vice versa.

3. A measure of how well the line fits the set of points through which it has been drawn. This measure is called the coefficient of determination and gives us a clue as to how trustworthy is our assumption that there is an association between our variables.

Regression analysis allows for the possibility of deriving more than one association among a number of potential influences. Such a possibility is in keeping with how we often read a situation. For example, in a comparison of observers, we might want to explore what features about them or about the conditions of their observing contribute to the correlation between their observations. Does length of experience in observation make their results more likely to agree? Does the length of video strip selected for them to analyze make a difference to the agreement? Or the nature of what they are asked to observe? Or do all three variables, experience, length of video strip and nature of observation, contribute to the degree of association?

The contributions of these further variables are added to the original equation and new regression coefficients are found. The equation can now no longer be represented by a line on a sheet of paper but by a line in multidimensional space with separate slopes for each new variable. These slopes or coefficients indicate the extent of the part played by each variable in the overall pattern of association.

EXERCISE TWELVE

In a case control study, outline the steps you would take to estimate how much significance you should attach to an established difference between the mean of the test group and the mean of the control group in your sample. (For suggestions see p.107.)

C. Presenting the findings

In research approaches that lie to the art work end of the spectrum, presenting our findings is one of those occasions when we can often enjoy a choice in how to proceed as regards both content and form.

A psychotherapist gives a detailed account of a case she has treated. She traces the origins and transformations of a symptom in chronological sequence from a traumatic event (which occurred when the patient was eighteen months old) and from parallel transference and counter-transference events in the here-and-now of therapy.

An art therapist describes as vignettes the changes she noticed in five cases of bipolar depression. She singles out the features that were common to all five (corroborating) and the features that some showed and others did not (cross-case analysis).

A consultant gives a sequential account of her work with a clinic for drug abuse, detailing the improvements in care, efficiency, and cost effectiveness.

These presentations follow a linear-analytic model (see Yin 1994, pp.136–141). The findings are displayed as events occurring one after the other in real time. The analysis accompanies this sequence, though of course it may refer (when appropriate) to the past.

Other models are available, especially for case studies. Sacks, in a series of dramatic instances, draws us along with the magnetism of a detective story (see Sacks 1995). Some occasions seem to invite the use of 'suspense':

A client hands a counsellor in mediation and divorce a lawyer's letter stating that divorce proceedings have now been started. A *fait accompli*. When the counsellor comes to write the case up for her dissertation, she imagines herself like a detective arriving at the scene of the crime, and working back from there. How did the couple reach the point of annulling a marriage of some forty years standing? She sifts the evidence with them for each stage in the dissolution of the marriage. Both partners agreed (for different reasons) that what all three called the 'suspense' approach was a good preparation for life after divorce.

And here, is an example of the 'comparative' model:

A music therapist records a series of improvisations taken in two contrasting groups, starting from the same motive and diverging according to mood, style, and group dynamic. He focused on the contrast, and presented his findings as two (metaphorical) columns.

So far the findings have been presented as realistic descriptions. Other stylistic genres may be tapped: the confessional, for example, or the impressionistic (see further Van Maanen 1988; Okely and Callaway 1992). The closer the presentation moves towards the art work pole of the spectrum of research approaches, the wider the range of styles that can be tried.

In a phenomenological study, a drama therapist wants to convey the force of feeling that, among several patients, lies behind the experience of being sexually abused as a child. He turns into first person the third person controlled narratives of his notebooks. Point after point springs into life.

In experimental studies, the presentation is usually determined by the design and is therefore straightforward provided the analysis has been carried out thoroughly. What is required is an unambiguous display of the findings and the conditions under which these findings were obtained. Since the findings are often couched in quantitative terms, tables and graphs are favoured. Comparative measures such as percentages and quartiles (see Altman and Bland 1994e) must be clearly defined in the presentation.

In a single case (N=1) study, the sequence of changes in outcome measures between periods of intervention and non-intervention may best be set out as a graph along the lines of a time series. In studies investigating differences in the outcomes of a control or experimental group, tables and graphs may assist in pointing up the contrasts. Similarly, graphs may be invaluable in illustrating multivariate clusters, correlations, and linear regressions. (For a brief review of the influence of electronic data bases and statistical packages on the mode of presentation see Lewith and Aldridge 1993, p.454.)

At the back of your mind constantly when you are considering how to present your experimental findings·should be two questions: what are the main points from my findings that I am trying to get across? What are the main points the reader will want to know? Sackett and Cook for example summarise the main points a practising doctor will want to glean from a research paper in terms of the efficacy and risks involved. (See further Sackett and Cook 1994).

Our findings (the notes, recordings, tables, analyzed results) become our data-base. Though often forming the core of our dissertation, the evidence in our data-base is usually separable from the final report, and as such may sometimes serve as a separate starting point for someone else's dissertation.

> S.G.Morton, a Philadelphian physician, included his raw data in a paper he wrote claiming black people had smaller cranial capacity than whites. S.J.Gould, re-analyzing the data one hundred and thirty years later, found no grounds to support the claim. (Davey-Smith 1994)

Davey-Smith goes on to list the advantages of a separate and shareable data-base: more efficient use of resources; confirmation or, as in the above example, correction of earlier conclusions; refinement of research questions and designs; enlarged data-sets and linkages; the possibility of meta-analyses. In medical research, the growth of a data-base such as the Cochrane Collaboration with its worldwide coverage sets a landmark on our journey towards knowing better what has been found. (See further Lilford 1994. Godlee 1994). At this stage, you need to be aware of this global potential, as well as the problems that remain over the exact level of what can be shared (the raw or the analyzed data) along with ethical issues over rights of transfer.

How you distribute the data-base across your final product, whether as part of the text, as a separate appendix, or as an unpublished wad retained in your notebook for a future occasion, rests on repeated decisions you make as the work progresses.

(ii) Discussing the findings

When our findings have been collected, analyzed, and presented, we are ready to assess their meaning and implications. In the first part of the discussion, we are likely to be concerned with relating our findings to what has gone before: particularly to the questions and topic covered in the Introduction (Cf Harris 1986, p.65) and to the issues raised in the Literature Review.

> The music therapist who began to explore how his patients used musical space in their improvisations (see pp.6–7) found his phenomenological approach supported and expanded by his readings in the journals of musical analysis, psychotherapy, and neurology. In his discussion, he was much taken up with illustrating the way his reading and his practice played into each other.

At this point too, it is worth reviewing the criteria on the basis of which we have interpreted our findings and the theory (or model) which informs these criteria.

Have our findings diverged appreciably from our original intention? The discussion section at the end of the findings is the appropriate place to show that you are aware of any such divergence and to explain its implications and how you have coped with it. An aspect of this divergence may have to do with the work of others. Where do our findings confirm those of others? where do they conflict with those of others?

> In a heuristic study about staying with a painful experience, a psychotherapist compares her own thresholds of pain with descriptions from others. She draws strength from certain common features that

caused others to feel pain, and the various ploys they adopt for resisting the urge to run away from pain. In her discussion section, she lists these common features and ploys, enlarges on their theoretical significance, and illustrates where she diverged from them.

Second, in discussing our findings, it may be appropriate to enlarge on a number of areas where certainty turns to doubt. In one sense, the keener your scientific honesty, the more these areas are likely to occur to you. To list a few that have cropped up in the course of this book:

- the various biases that keep slipping in behind our backs (bias on the part of therapists wanting to prove their treatment effective, wanting their patients to get well; bias on the part of patients wanting to improve, wanting to please or thwart their therapists); the placebo effect (Lewith and Aldridge 1993, Chapter 4);

- the sensitivity or otherwise of our instruments, and the corresponding false positives or false negatives that slip through (Altman and Bland 1994c and 1994d);

- the hidden effect of a statistically recognised phenomenon such as regression towards the mean (Altman and Bland 1994b. Fleminger 1994), not to mention the constant eruptions of chance; generalizability;

- causes and associations. (Causality is only one out of four inferences we may draw from the occurrence of an association. The other three possible inferences would be that the two associated variables are simply caught up with each other, as the rotation of one wheel of a car is caught up with and closely correlated with the rotation of the three other wheels; that the two associated variables are related to a third variable; that the two variables are associated by coincidence, whatever we mean by that.)

These and many issues like them may need an airing in the discussion if you've come up against them in the course of your observations.

Third, the discussion is the place to forestall criticism by getting your retaliation in first. Go through your arguments and consider other possible explanations, their strengths and weaknesses and why you have rejected them, if only for the moment.

A final point. There are no hard and fast rules about the distribution of the discussion across the dissertation. Each lay out has to be decided on its own merits.

A student found 'discussion' entering into his dissertation at a number of points: in the elicitation of data (he used several small group discussions based on five selected questions); in the discussion about the data; in the conclusions. The topic of the dissertation was 'Finding your shadow'. The questions he particularly addressed in himself and to his respondents concerned the complement, the inverse, of various positions. In the discussion about the data, the student sought to set these questions in a wider theoretical frame: what is the relation of shadow to 'substance', to identity, to self? Shadow, complements, inverses, all imply a dualism. What are the implications of dualism? How does dualism relate to 'single-mindedness', to purpose, to getting something done, to deciding on what is better or worse? There was something about the topic of the thesis that led repeatedly to divergence into discussion.

CHAPTER VII

Conclusions and the Abstract

1. *In what way is your dissertation distinctive? How might you increase its distinction? Its authority?*

2. *Does your dissertation convey a sense of completeness?*

3. *Have you clearly defined the boundaries within the topic and between the topic and other related areas?*

4. *Have you collected, distilled, and displayed the relevant evidence?*

5. *What measures have you taken to enhance your awareness of alternative perspectives? Have you given enough space in the dissertation to alternative perspectives?*

6. *Can you define gaps in your own work? or areas which bring your own ideas into conflict with others? Do these gaps and conflicting areas suggest trying a shift across the spectrum of research approaches? Or do they suggest new fields into which you might move?*

7. *Does your presentation engage, entice, and seduce the reader?*

8. *What are some of the problems you envisage having to face when you come to implement your research? What steps might you take to deal with these problems?*

In conclusions, we consider:

(i) checks and balances.

(ii) a list of the main points established and the gaps that remain.

(iii) future steps envisaged.

(iv) the abstract.

(v) implementing the research.

(i) Checks and balances

By the time we reach the conclusions, our dissertation has become the object we can review in the same way that we looked at others' work in the literature review. (See chapter V.) The criteria listed there we may now apply to our own work: the checks for adequate coverage, for 'completeness', for bias, for sound inferences and chains of argument, for validity and reliability.

These criteria should be addressed to the overall research design, which is concerned with the interrelation of all the ingredients in our dissertation. Here is an outline of the overall research design:

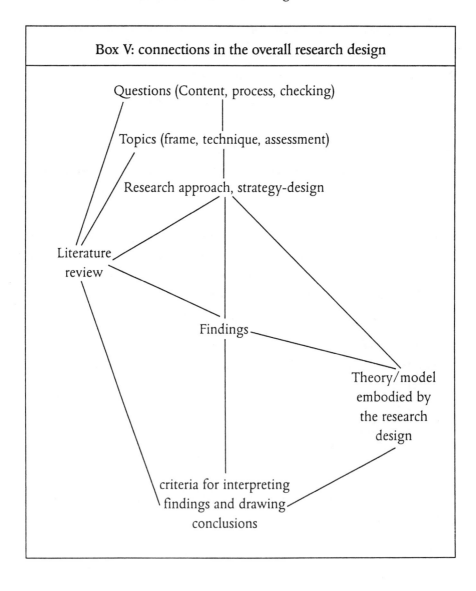

Box V: connections in the overall research design

Questions (Content, process, checking)

Topics (frame, technique, assessment)

Research approach, strategy-design

Literature review

Findings

Theory/model embodied by the research design

criteria for interpreting findings and drawing conclusions

Each step in the route from questions to conclusions should be checked:

- Have you asked the right questions, clearly and unambiguously?
- Do the questions adequately address and cover the topic?
- Have you given your topic clear boundaries?
- Have you described adequately your research approach and design?
- If patients are involved, have you given full consideration to their condition and respected all the ethical guidelines?
- Are your findings credible and relevant to the question(s) posed?
- Are they well and clearly presented, providing all necessary information for readers to form their judgements?
- Are your interpretations and conclusions warranted by your findings, and well argued speculations?
- Have you married your findings to available and appropriate theoretical models?
- Have you covered the relevant literature and paid sufficient attention to the work, arguments and conclusions of others, especially when these may differ from your own?

Brenda, a nursing counsellor, was reading through her dissertation on 'The epidemiology of the Crack syndrome'. She was underlining the main conclusions from the analysis, discussion, and summary. She suddenly noticed that in two conclusions she was assuming a population whose boundaries lay beyond those of the population being investigated. These two as yet unjustified conclusions pointed to a gap not only in her own study but also in papers covered in her review of the literature. She therefore transferred these two conclusions to the section in her dissertation where she was addressing future steps. She outlined there how the population would have to be enlarged if these extended generalizations were to be tested.

Watch for points where deductive logic falters.

Bill, a movement therapist, based several conclusions in his dissertation on the assumption that, since he hadn't found any response to a particular technique, no such response could possibly exist. A

mathematical colleague, versed in logic, pointed out that no evidence
of an effect was not the same as evidence, let alone proof, of no effect.
After an ill-tempered wrangle, Bill toned down the certainty of his
negative assertions.

If you are using quantitative assessments, you will need to watch out for many
traps. To give one example, be wary how you interpret the results of sub
group analyses, such as analyzing the results obtained from one sex only, in
a heterosexual sample. (In the BMJ (1995) 310:52–3, there is a useful
check-list for the statistically minded covering design features, conduct of
study, analysis and presentation.)

(ii) The main points established

Our conclusions flow directly from the discussion section of the findings and
the final review of the research design. You will need to:

1. List carefully every point you have established, setting each in a logical
   context with what has been established already. (The exception here
   may be art work where the revelatory impact of any conclusion is
   immediate and wrapped up in the presentation).

2. Distinguish where at any point on this list you have broken into new
   ground (modifying previous models or extending generalizations) and
   where you are replicating previous work. (see further Harris 1986,
   p.66)

3. Identify the gaps that remain in your own work, linking these gaps with
   those you have noticed in others' work.

(iii) Future steps envisaged

The identification of gaps in our own and others' work leads to our outlining
future steps. What further projects does your dissertation suggest by way of
replication, filling out, or change of direction? Do you see yourself as
undertaking these further steps or do you envisage recruiting others?
    Your conclusions may point to a number of possibilities:

1. Moving across the spectrum of research approaches eg from a
   phenomenological case report to an experimental single case (N=1)
   study.

2. Extending generalizations e.g. by undertaking a series of case reports.

3. Modifying the theoretical model.

4. Trying other fields.

These possibilities are closely linked with how a research project grows, changing through a number of stages that may well continue for years. (For a useful review of these stages see Harris 1986 and on a larger scale Reason and Rowan 1981). The growth entails several circular processes. The **first** is between

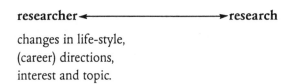

researcher ← → research

changes in life-style,
(career) directions,
interest and topic.

The **second** circular process is between complementary changes inherent in the growth of research itself (cf the contrary, complementary, poles that informed the spectrum of research approaches). Practice and research, as we have seen, go together as complementary moves. More generally, Gregory suggests that in research itself, there are two modes of thinking: the rapid intuitive mode which results in 'hand-waving' explanations; and the slow sequential mode, which he calls 'handle-turning' (Gregory 1992). Along similar lines, Bateson and others have suggested that all advance in creative thought and experience proceeds by the alternation of 'loose' and 'tight' thinking (Bateson 1973). In research we need both the 'hand-waving' loose-thinking modes of experience (Medawar's 'imaginative exploit of the single mind') and the 'handle-turning', tight-thinking modes (Medawar's testing by experiment, that 'ruthlessly critical process to which many skills and many hands are lent'. See Cooper 1991).

Here then the circle is between

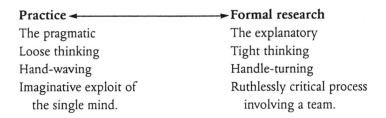

Practice ←	→ Formal research
The pragmatic	The explanatory
Loose thinking	Tight thinking
Hand-waving	Handle-turning
Imaginative exploit of	Ruthlessly critical process
the single mind.	involving a team.

Through assessing the effects of treatment (practice), we often move circularly into formulating the problem and sharpening our model more precisely (research). (See further Heal and Wigram 1993, Chapter 20). Through the relatively 'loose-thinking' of a case-study we might move into the 'tighter' thinking of an experimental research design based on a single case which provides its own control (see pp.59–61).

A **third** circular process in the growth of a research project is that between the (apparently) simple and the complex, or between the (apparently) concrete and the abstract. (We've already met this process when touching on the relation between art work and maths work. See pp.56–57). Research studies where the design is kept simple, and the corresponding limitations are recognised, can be valuable both in their own right and in the preparation they provide for more elaborate and costly designs. (See further Lewith and Aldridge 1993, Chapter 11.)

So you might consider generalizing your present conclusions by extending your initial hermeneutic case report or N=1 case study into a series. (See for example the links between N=1 case studies and a randomized double blind prospective controlled trial in March *et al.* 1994). Or you might consider convening several small groups to discuss various issues raised in a phenomenological case report. In this further step, you might aim to isolate key areas for a more complex testing.

One type of such complex testing might be a controlled survey. Another type might be one of the more elaborate experimental studies touched on when we were looking at the range of research strategies and designs. Conklin, for example, speaks of the phases in ethnographic research that range from everyday conversations in which the analysis of various verbal techniques may be employed, through the making of films, to the quantification of data, and the critical and probabilistic changes in the microsocial environment (Conklin 1968). Sometimes the growth is in the opposite direction: qualitative research is needed to bolster quantitative findings (Chapman 1993). We should be wary of any hierarchical view that conceives the quantitative handling of qualitative measures as somehow a superior exercise (see further in Yin 1994, p.3). On the integration of qualitative and quantitative methods, see Pope and May 1993, and Krause 1994. For a good description of research as a circular developmental process, drawing on a variety of qualitative and quantitative approaches, see Lewith and Aldridge 1993, Chapters 17 and 18.

iv) The abstract

Some writers like to map out their abstract from the start. They find it gives them a useful corset within which to work. If the abstract begins to bulge unduly, they know they're in difficulties with their overall design.

More usually, the abstract is the last section to be written. BUT IT IS ALWAYS THE FIRST TO APPEAR. This privileged position in the sequence of presentation is what gives the abstract its peculiar importance.

Although less than 500 words, the abstract carries more clout than all the rest of the dissertation put together. For one simple reason. Given the eruption of information technology, and the corresponding reduction of attention span, the abstract is likely to be the only section of your dissertation that the vast majority of readers will scan. Will they get from it the gist of what you have done?

The abstract is the equivalent of the opening sentence in any piece of writing. Does it hook the reader or not?

In the abstract, we have to epitomise the five steps in any research:

Box VI: headings for the abstract

- how and why did we start on it?
- what is our central question and topic?
- how did we go about tackling it?
- what did we find?
- what did it mean and what did we conclude?

There is room only for the bare essential details. No afterthoughts. No obscurities.

The chosen research approach and design of the dissertation will inevitably shape the abstract. An experimental approach will entail a summary of objective, research design, setting, participants, interventions, outcome measures, results and conclusions (see for example the lay out of abstracts in the British Medical Journal. Also Hurth 1987). Less formal approaches may allow fewer subheadings.

The key is to be concise and entice.

In fact, one last reminder, before submitting the final draft, **go through the manuscript, and trim the writing**, for pace, clarity, and form. Iron out ambiguities:

> An art therapist was reading through a colleague's draft. She came upon the sentence: 'The proportion of depressives in the test group was one in ten. It was half that in the control group.' What, she wondered, was the proportion in the control group? One in five or one in twenty?

Shorten the sentences, enliven with verbs and sharp visual imagery (see further Albert 1992).

EXERCISE THIRTEEN

> Trim the following second paragraph in the Introduction in a dissertation on 'Tempo in therapy'.

> > 'In this dissertation, as we have already implied, the main idea of the study as it evolved was the examination of the association between patient and therapists' rhythm (more specifically the rhythmic beat, or rather the pace of the beat, the tempo) and the exploration of what eventuates in therapy when some resonance or perhaps better synchronous exchange is established in tempo between patient and therapist. These are the questions we have endeavoured to bear in mind as the foundation on which this study is based.' (Suggested answer p.107)

(v) Implementation

Your dissertation by now is the image with which you can continue to have a dialogue and through which others can have a dialogue with you:

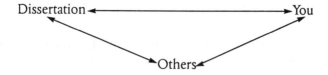

This is the start of implementing your research, the point at which it turns into action research. How are you going to apply your ideas and ensure they gain greater authority and influence? (For more on developments in action research see Miller 1993 especially where he notes the circular connection between roles and theoretical constructs among those action researchers involved in the 'laboratory of real life'.)

One benefit of this dialogue is the opportunity it affords us to hear from others and to assess the alternative perspectives that may be gleaned from colleagues, informants, patients (Lansdown 1994), students (MacManus *et al.* 1993), and a wider audience once we publish our findings. (See further the importance of follow up letters on research papers in Bhopal and Tonks 1994).

The wider the audience, the fuller and better informed the reviews (Cf Smith 1992b). Hence among the first and crucial steps in implementing your findings is the need to get published with all that entails for networking and tapping into further research resources. (See further some practical hints in Aldridge and Lewith 1993, pp.459–72 on applying for research grants).

Once published you are into the field of audit. With research we are concerned with discovering the right thing to do; with audit, we are concerned with ensuring it gets done (Smith 1992a, Crossley *et al.* 1992, Russell and Wing 1992, Peter 1993, Williams *et al.* 1992). The field is beset with problems and challenges.

First another circular process

What are we doing?⟵————————⟶what should we be doing?
(Bhopal and Thomson 1991)

Second, do we know with any precision, what we and others are doing, let alone what we should be doing? This raises the whole question of co-ordinating and assessing competent research. (See for example the Cochrane Collaboration in Chalmers *et al.* 1992. Cf the collaboration of arts therapists noted in Lewith and Aldridge 1992, p.475).

Third, even when we know what we should be doing, how effectively are relevant research conclusions finding their way into practice? What influence is good research having on the education and practice of those delivering the services from which it was drawn? In medicine, there are suggestions of a considerable gap (Smith 1993 and 1994a, Channer 1994, Haines and Jones 1994).

Fourth, how far can we intervene effectively in people's wish to change (Stott *et al.* 1994)? How is any influence we may seek to exert best channelled? Many controversies surround the role of guide lines (Feder 1994).

Small wonder that the ethics and politics of what is involved in implementing research is exercising the minds of planners up to the highest level. You need to know about these challenges if you are to cope with them after your own fashion, and do justice to the hours you've put into reaching this point in the book.

Answers to Exercises

EXERCISE ONE (p.4)

Some suggested questions may be as follows:

1. What are the possible changes in my skin that might be measured? Humidity in the skin? Sweat? Skin temperature? (Static) electricity? Skin biochemistry? Hormonal mechanisms?

2. What is the marker designed to be measuring? What model was suggested to explain the marker's changes of colour? How does this model correspond with other models set up for measuring skin changes associated with stress?

3. What in the marker are the mechanisms that cause it to register changes in its environment? Are these changes it's registering the same as those it's supposed to be measuring?

4. Was the marker responding to me at all? Were the influences it was recording impinging on its upper rather than its lower (myskin) side?

5. What tests have been done to validate the claims of these markers?

EXERCISE TWO (p.10)

Yes, if repetition is seen as part of a spiral, i.e. as involving change since the context in which the repetition occurs, has changed. Yes, if as part of a pulse or metre, repetition is seen as a necessary component of rhythm. Bruscia includes repetition (of melody or rhythm) as a technique for eliciting a musical response or for establishing an emotional climate or mood. He notes the connections between repetition, expectation, change, and predictability (Bruscia 1987, p.543). Yes, if repetition is a form of replication (see later in Chapter VI on 'reliability' p.83) No, if the same point is being made in different, and still more so in the same, words. In your dissertation, you need to watch out for repetition, and either justify as above, or discard.

EXERCISE THREE (p.15)

The question would involve you in defining: arts therapy; cure; depression (including such issues as cross-cultural definitions and rating scales).

EXERCISE SIX (p.33)

The short answer is that any such evaluation is impossible. A longer answer and one more sympathetic to the calls of scepticism, and economic planners ('why should we grant you money for an exercise whose effectiveness you haven't proved?') would have to assess the nature and quality of the work itself; the measurable benefits it may bring to patients and staff; the cultural climate (including landscape and curriculum) with which it intermeshes. (See further Miles, 1994).

EXERCISE SEVEN (p.47)

Another apparently simple question where the answers can easily become a book. Some of the points to be covered: effect (anything between dramatic or apparently none) of the interpretation on patient, therapist and relation between the two; enhancing or blocking understanding; over time (how long? and how do you map the changes?); in context (how can you decide what bit of the interpretation or whether it was the interpretation at all which had any effect? or what bit of the effect?).

EXERCISE EIGHT (p.53)

Homeopathy at present lies outside the traditional Western medical rubric as taught in established medical schools. In examining its effectiveness, we run into similar difficulties to those we encounter when we try to assess medical systems from other cultures, or complementary therapies in our own. These difficulties include separating part from whole both in the receiver and what is received. Suggestions for assessing complementary therapies are covered in Knipschild 1993, McGourty 1993, Holmes 1994, Marks 1994, Lewith and Aldridge 1993, Chapters 8 and 9. Specific issues relating to homeopathy are covered in Lewith and Aldridge 1993 Chapters 22, 24, and 25, Buckman and Lewith 1994, Kleijnen *et al.* 1991. Cf also McQuay and Moore 1994, McWhinney *et al.* 1994.

EXERCISE NINE (p.67)

The therapist would need to relate at least three complex sequences: the process of cancer, which increasingly seems linked with a chain of biochemical changes and immunity: the process of depression, which goes with basic psychological patterns such as the inturning of aggression; the process of divorce, which, by definition, is tied up with the long-standing quality of a marriage (including illusions and projective identifications). In the case she was treating, all three processes were at work and any simple equation between one and another (e.g. divorce=cancer) should ring a loud warning bell in her sceptical sub-personality.

EXERCISE TWELVE (p.89)
Steps should include:

1. Respecting conditions for collecting your sample e.g. size, and representativeness.

2. Ensuring homogeneity, matching, and where feasible randomisation of the two groups.

3. Determining the mean of the test group and the mean of the control group and the difference between the two means.

4. Determining the standard error of the difference between the the two means.

5. Using inferential statistics to calculate the degree of probability, and the confidence interval for this standard error of difference between the two means, in a sample of this size. (See further Gardner and Altman 1989, and Gardner, Gardner and Winter 1991.)

EXERCISE THIRTEEN (p.102)
Something along the lines of: The questions addressed in this dissertation are:

(1) How does the therapist respond to the patient's tempo?

(2) What is the effect of this response on treatment?

References

Agar, M. (1980) *The Professional Stranger*. New York: Academic Press.

Albert, T. (1992) *Medical Journalism: The Writer's Guide*. Oxford: Radcliffe Medical Press.

Altman, D.G. (1994) 'The scandal of poor medical research.' *British Medical Journal 308*, 283–4.

Altman, D.G. and Bland, J.M. (1994a) 'Correlation, regression, and repeated data.' *British Medical Journal 308*, 896.

Altman, D.G. and Bland, J.M. (1994b) 'Regression towards the mean.' *British Medical Journal 308*, 1499.

Altman, D.G. and Bland, J.M. (1994c) 'Diagnostic tests I: sensitivity and specificity.' *British Medical Journal 308*, 1582.

Altman, D.G. and Bland, J.M. (1994d) 'One and two sided tests of significance.' *British Medical Journal 309*, 248.

Altman, D.G. and Bland, J.M. (1994e) 'Quartiles, quintiles, centiles and other quantiles.' *British Medical Journal 309*, 996.

Altman, D.G. and Bland, J.M. (1994f) 'Matching.' *British Medical Journal 309*, 1128.

Andersen, B. (1990) *Methodological Errors in Medical Research*. Oxford: Blackwell.

Atkinson, P. (1992) 'The ethnography of a medical setting: reading, writing, and rhetoric.' *Qualitative Health Research 2*, 451–74.

Barlow, J. (1992) 'University research outlook.' Letter to *Financial Times* 31.10.92.

Bartal, L. and Ne'eman, N. (1993) *The Metaphoric Body: Guide to Expressive Therapy Through Images and Archetypes*. London: Jessica Kingsley Publishers.

Bateson, G. (1973) *Steps to an Ecology of the Mind*. New York: Jason Aronson.

Begley, S. (1992) 'Maths has Pi on its face.' *Newsweek* 7.12.94.

Bell, J. (1993) *Doing your Research Project: A Guide for First-Time Researchers in Education and Social Science*. Milton Keynes: Open University Press.

Berrios, G.E. (1989) 'What is phenomenology? a review.' *Journal of the Royal Society of Medicine 82*, 425–28.

Bettelheim, B. (1983) *Freud and Man's Soul*. London: Chatto and Windus.

Bhopal, R.S. and Thompson, R. (1991) 'A form to help learn and teach about assessing medical audit papers.' *British Medical Journal 303*, 1520–2.

Bhopal, R.S. and Tonks, A. (1994) 'The role of letters in reviewing research.' *British Medical Journal 308*, 1582–3.

Brandon, S. (1991) 'Ethics, economics, and science.' *Journal of the Royal Society of Medicine 84*, 575–7.

Brennan, P. and Croft, P. (1994) 'Interpreting the results of observational research: chance is not such a fine thing.' *British Medical Journal 309*, 727–30.

Bridgeman, P. (1950) *Reflections of a Physicist.* New York: Philosophical Library.

Bruscia, K.E. (1987) *Improvisational Models of Music Therapy.* Springfield, Illinois: Charles C Thomas.

Buber, M. (1965) *The Knowledge of Man.* New York: Harper and Row.

Buck, D. and Sutton, M. (1994) 'Problems with confounders can be tackled.' *British Medical Journal 309*, 1439.

Buckman, R. and Lewith, G. (1994) 'What does homeopathy do and how?' *British Medical Journal 309*, 103–6.

Bullock, A., Stallybrass, O. and Trombley, S. (eds) (1988) *The Fontana Dictionary of Modern Thought.* London: Fontana Press.

Carrithers, M. (1992) *Why Humans have Cultures; Explaining Anthropology and Social Diversity.* Oxford: Oxford University Press.

Chalmers, I,. Dickersin, K. and Chalmers, T.C. (1992) 'Getting to grips with Archie Cochrane's agenda.' *British Medical Journal 305:*, 786–7.

Chalmers, I. and Haynes, B. (1994) 'Reporting, updating, and correcting systematic reviews of the effects of health care.' *British Medical Journal 309*, 862–5.

Channer, K.S. (1994) 'Auditing the British Medical Journal.' *Journal of the Royal Society of Medicine 87*, 655–7.

Chapman, S. (1993) 'Unravelling gossamer with boxing gloves: problems in explaining the decline in smoking.' *British Medical Journal 307*, 429–32.

Chodorow, J. (1991) *Dance Therapy and Depth Psychology: The Moving Imagination.* London: Routledge.

Clarke, J.J. (1994) 'Jung and Eastern Thought: A Dialogue with the Orient. London and New York: Routledge.

Clarke, M.J. and Stewart, L.A. (1994) 'Obtaining data from randomised control trials: how much do we need for reliable and informative meta-analyses?' *British Medical Journal 309*, 1007–9.

Conklin, H.C. (1968) 'Ethnography.' Article in *International encyclopedia of social science V*, 172–8. New York: Macmillan and Free Press.

Cookson, C. (1994) 'New conclusions from old studies.' *Financial Times.* 6.11.94.

Cooper, W. (1991) 'Peter Medawar.' *Independent Magazine.* 2.11.91.

Cornwell, A. and Lindisfarne, N. (1994) *Dislocating Masculinity; Comparative Ethnographies.* London and New York: Routledge.

Counsell, C.E., Clarke, M.J., Slattery, J. and Sandercock, A.G. (1994) 'The miracle of DICE therapy for acute stroke: fact or fictional product of subgroup analysis.' *British Medical Journal 309*, 1677–81.

Crossley, D., Myres, M.P. and Wilkinson, P. (1992) 'Assessment of psychological care in general practice.' *British Medical Journal 305*, 1333–6.

Davey Smith, G. (1994) 'Increasing the accessibility of data.' *British Medical Journal 308*, 1519–20.

Davey Smith, G. and Phillips, A.N. (1992) 'Confounding in epidemiological studies: why independent effects may not be all they seem.' *British Medical Journal 305*, 757–9.

Delamothe, T. (1994) 'Using outcomes research in clinical practice.' *British Medical Journal 308*, 1583–4.

Devish, R. and Vervaeck, B. (1986) 'Doors and thresholds: Jeddi's approach to psychiatric disorders.' *Soc.Sci.Med 22*, 541–51.

Dickersin, K., Scherer, R. and Lefebvre, C. (1994) 'Identifying relevant studies for systematic reviews.' *British Medical Journal 309*, 1286–91.

Doll, R. (1992) 'Sir Austin Bradford Hill and the progress of medical science.' *British Medical Journal 305*, 1521–6.

Eliade, M. (1974) 'The Myth of the Eternal Return or Cosmos and History. Princeton, New Jersey: Princeton University Press.

Eliot, T.S. (1978) The Waste Land. In *The Complete Poems and Plays of T.S. Eliot*. London: Faber and Faber.

Eysenck H.J. (1994) 'Meta-analysis and its problems.' *British Medical Journal 309*, 789–92.

Feder, G. (1994) 'Clinical guidelines in 1994: let's be careful out there.' *British Medical Journal 309*, 1457–8.

Field, N. (1994) 'Object relations and individuation.' *Journal of Analytical Psychology 39*, 463–79.

Fleminger, S. (1994) 'Follow-up letter to Altman and Bland 1994(b).' *British Medical Journal 309*, 539.

Forinash, M. (1993) 'An exploration into qualitative research in music therapy.' *Arts in Psychotherapy 20*, 69–73.

Fowler, F.G.R. and Fulton, P.M. (1991) 'Critical appraisal of published research.' *British Medical Journal 302*, 1136–40.

Gadamer, H-G. (1975) *Truth and Method*. London: Sheed and Ward.

Gardner, M.J. and Altman, D.G. (1989) *Statistics with Confidence*. London: British Medical Journal Publications.

Gardner, M.J., Gardner, S.B. and Winter, P.D. (1991) *Confidence Interval Analysis (CIA): Microcomputer Program Manual*. London: British Medical Journal Publications.

Garner, P. Torres, T.T. and Alonso, P. (1994) 'Trial design in developing countries.' *British Medical Journal 309*, 825–6.

Godlee, F. (1994) 'The Cochrane Collaboration.' *British Medical Journal 309*, 969–70.

Greene, J. and D'Oliveira, M. (1989) *Learning to use Statistical Tests in Psychology: A Student's Guide.* Milton Keynes: Open University Press.

Greene, R.J. and Maklan, C.W. (1994) 'Research into outcomes and effectiveness.' Letter in reply to Sheldon 1994. *British Medical Journal 309*, 878–9.

Gregory, R. (1992) 'The art of science.' An interview with Christian Tyler in the *Financial Times* 15.2.92.

Groves, B. (1994) 'Fallacies that can be fatal in medical matters.' Article in *Financial Times* 7.12.94. following up Cookson 1994.

Haines, A. and Jones, R. (1994) 'Implementing findings of research.' *British Medical Journal 308*, 1488–92.

Hall, G.M. (ed) (1994) *How to Write a Paper.* London: British Medical Journal Publishing Group.

Hammersley, M. and Atkinson, P. (1983) *Ethnography: Principles in Practice.* London: Tavistock Publications.

Happold, F.C. (1970) *Mysticism: A Study and an Anthology.* Quotation from Max Planck's autobiography. London: Penguin Books.

Harris, P. (1986) *Designing and Reporting Experiments.* Milton Keynes: Open University Press.

Harris Williams, M. and Waddell, M. (1991) *The Chamber of Maiden Thought.* Chapter 5 on Coleridge. London: Routledge.

Hashim, A. (1994) 'An incident that influenced my life.' *British Medical Journal 309*, 779.

Hayslett, H.T. and Murphy, P. (1979) *Statistics made Simple.* London: W.H.Allen.

Heal, M.H. and Wigram, T. (1993) *Music Therapy in Health and Education.* London: Jessica Kingsley Publishers.

Herxheimer, A. (1991) 'Challenge for clinical trialists.' *British Medical Journal 303*, 1076.

Herxheimer, A. (1995) 'These drug wars are for real.' *The Guardian* 25.1.95.

Higgins, R. (1993) *Approaches to Case Study.* London: Jessica Kingsley Publishers.

Higgins, R. (1994) Postural Change. Unpublished paper.

Hillman, J. (1983) *Healing Fiction.* New York: Station Hill Press.

Hinshelwood, R.D. (1989) *A Dictionary of Kleinian Thought.* London: Free Association Books.

Hinshelwood, R.D. (1991) 'Psychodynamic formulation in assessment for psychotherapy.' *British Journal of Psychotherapy 8*, 166–.

Hofstadter, D.R. (1979) *Gödel, Escher, Bach: An Eternal Gold Braid.* London: Penguin.

Holmes, J. (1994) 'Psychotherapy, a luxury the NHS cannot afford? more expensive not to treat.' *British Medical Journal 309*, 1070–1.

Holub, M. (1990) *The Dimension of the Present Moment.* (Translation by Young D). Essay on Poetry and science. London: Faber and Faber.

Hospers, J. (1967) *Introduction to Philosophical Analysis.* London: Routledge and Kegan Paul.

Hughes, C.C. (1992) 'Ethnography: what's in a word_ process? product? promise?' *Qualitative health research 2*, 439–50.

Hurth, E.J. (1987) 'Structured abstracts for papers reporting clinical trials.' *Ann.int.med. 106*, 626–7.

Jaspers, K. (1913) (Translated 1963 by Hoenig J and Hamilton M.W.from 7th German edition). *General Psychopathology.* Manchester: Manchester University Press.

Johnson, R.A. (1991) *Owning your Own Shadow.* New York: Harper Collins.

Joseph, A.B. and Young, J.J. (1992) *Movement Disorders in Neurology and Neuropsychiatry.* Especially chapters 47 and 49. New York: Blackwells.

Jung, C.J. (1953–83) *Collected Works.* (Eds Read H. Fordham M. and Adler G. Translated by Hull R.F.C.). Vol.18. London: Routledge.

Junge, M.B. and Linesch, D. (1993) 'Our own voices: new paradigms for art therapy research.' *Arts in Psychotherapy 20*, 61–7.

Kasayka, R. (1991) To meet and match the moment of hope: transpersonal elements of the guided imagery and music experience. Unpublished documentary dissertation. Quoted in Forinash 1993.

Kazdin, A.E. (1982) *Single-Case Research Designs.* Oxford: Oxford University Press.

Kennedy, A.C. (1991) 'Discovery in medicine.' *British Medical Journal 303*, 1569–72.

Kleijnen, J., Knipschild, P. ter Riet G. (1991) 'Clinical trials of homeopathy.' *British Medical Journal 302*, 316–23.

Kline, M. (1953) *Mathematics in Western Culture.* London: Pelican.

Knipschild, P. (1993) 'Trials and errors. Alternative thoughts on the methodology of clinical trials.' *British Medical Journal 306*, 1706–7.

Kramer, M.S. and Shapiro, S.H. (1987) 'Scientific challenges in the application of randomised trials.' *J.Am.Med.Assn. 252*, 2739–63.

Kraupl Taylor, F. (1967) 'The role of phenomenology in psychiatry.' *British Journal of Psychiatry 113*, 765–70.

Krause, I-B. (1994) 'Numbers and meaning: a dialogue in cross-cultural psychiatry.' *Journal of the Royal Society for Medicine 87*, 278–82.

Lansdown, R.J. (1994) 'Does doctor know best? Patient input into medical decision making.' *Journal of the Royal Society for Medicine 87*, 716–7.

Lancaster, T. (1993) 'A book that changed my practice. Weighing the evidence.' *British Medical Journal 307*, 662.

Landy, R.J. (1993) 'Introduction: a research agenda for creative arts therapists.' *Arts in psychotherapy 20*, 1–2.

Lewith, G.T. and Aldridge, D. (1993) *Clinical Research Methodology for Complementary Therapies*. London: Hodder and Stoughton.

Lilford, R.J. (1994) 'The Cochrane pregnancy and childbirth database.' *British Medical Journal 308*, 1448.

Lock, S. and Wells, F. (eds) (1993) *Fraud and Misconduct in Medical Research*. London: British Medical Journal Publications.

Macbeth, F. (1994) 'Patients being unwilling to enter clinical trials.' Letter to the *British Medical Journal 309*, 539–40.

MacManus, I.C., Vincent, C.A., Thom, S. and Kidd, J. (1993) 'Teaching communications skills to clinical students.' *British Medical Journal 306*, 1322–7.

MacManus, I.C. (1994) 'Reply to Brennan and Croft 1994.' *British Medical Journal 309*, 1158.

McGourty, H. (1993) 'How to evaluate complementary therapies: a literature review.' Liverpool Public Health Observatory. Observatory report series No. 13.

McGrath, P. (1994) 'Tangled in the net.' *Newsweek* 16.12.94, p.38.

McNiff, S. (1993) 'The authority of experience.' *Arts in psychotherapy 20*, 3–9.

McQuay, H. and Moore, A. (1994) 'Need for rigorous assessment of palliative care.' *British Medical Journal 309*, 1315–6.

McWhinney, I.R., Bass, M.J. and Donner, A. (1994) 'Evaluation of a palliative care system: problems and pitfalls.' *British Medical Journal 309*, 1340–2.

Magee, B. (1987) *The Great Philosophers*. Especially chapter 12 on Husserl and Heidegger. London: BBC Books.

March, L., Irving, L., Schwarz, J., Simpson, J., Chock, C. and Brooks, P. (1994) 'N Of 1 trials comparing a non-steroidal anti-inflammatory drug with paracetomal in osteoarthritis.' *British Medical Journal 309*, 1041–6.

Marks, I. (1994) 'Unevaluated or inefficient approaches are hard to justify.' *British Medical Journal 309*, 1071–2.

Messiaen, O. (1944) *Technique of my Musical Language*. (Trans J. Satterfield.) Paris: Leduc.

Miles, M.F.R. (1994) 'Art in hospitals: does it work? A survey of evaluation of arts projects in the NHS.' *Journal of the Royal Society for Medicine 87*, 161–3.

Miller, A. (1994) 'Buried without a trace: the danger of censorship is in our collaboration.' *Wiener Zeitung* 20.5.94.

Miller, E.J. (1993) *From Dependency to Autonomy: Studies in Organisation and Change*. London: Free Association Books.

Moustakas, C. (1990) *Heuristic Research: Design, Methodology, and Application.* California and London: Sage Publications.

Nietzsche, F. (1984) *Human all too Human.* (Marion Faber trans. with Stephen Lehmann). Lincoln, New England: Univ. of Nebraska Press.

Nowak, R. (1994) 'Problems in clinical trials go far beyond misconduct.' *Science 264,* 1538–41.

Ogden, C.K. and Richards, I.A. (1946) *The Meaning of Meaning.* London: Kegan Paul, Trench, Trubner.

Okely, J. and Callaway, H. (1992) *Anthropology and Autobiography. London: Routledge.*

Orchard, C. (1994) 'Comparing health care outcomes.' *British Medical Journal 308,* 1493–6.

Oxman, A.D. (1994) 'Checklist for review articles.' *British Medical Journal 309,* 648–51.

Persaud, R. (1994) Follow up letter to Altman and Bland 1994(a) *British Medical Journal 308,* 1510.

Peter, L. (1993) 'Audit in primary care paediatrics.' *British Medical Journal 307,* 51–53.

Pike, K. (1967) Language in relation to a unified theory of the structure of human nature (The Hague) quoted in Seymour-Smith 1986.

Planck, M. See Happold (1970).

Pollock, A.V. (1993) 'Surgical evaluations at the cross-roads.' *British Journal of Surgery 80,* 964–6.

Pope, C. and May, N. (1993) 'Opening the black box: an encounter in the corridors of health services research.' *British Medical Journal 306,* 315–8.

Popper, K. (1934) (Translated into English 1959. Revised edition 1972) *The Logic of Scientific Discovery.* London: Hutchinson.

Reason, P. and Rowan, J. (1981) *Human Inquiry.* Chichester: John Wiley.

Ricoeur, P. (1978) *The Rule of Metaphor: Multi-Disciplinary Studies of the Creation of Meaning in Languagle.* Translated by Czerny R. London: Routledge and Kegan Paul.

Ricoeur, P. (1981) *Hermeneutics and the Human Science.* Cambridge: Cambridge University Press.

Rous, E. (1994) 'Letter addressing problems over funding in Smythe *et al.* 1994.' *British Medical Journal 309,* 741.

Russell, B. (1912) *Problems of Philosophy.* Oxford: Oxford University Press.

Russell, B. (1917) *Mysticism and Logic.* London: Allen and Unwin.

Russell, B. (1935) *Sceptical Essays.* London: Allen and Unwin.

Russell, B. (1949) *Scientific Outlook.* London: Allen and Unwin.

Russell, I. and Wing, D.K. (1992) 'Medical audit in general practice.' *British Medical Journal 304,* 1480–4.

Ruthven, K.K. (1976) *Myth*. London: Methuen.

Rycroft, C.F. (1985) *Psychoanalysis and Beyond*. London: Chatto and Windus.

Sacks, O. (1995) *An Anthropologist on Mars*. London: Picador.

Sackett, D.L. and Cook, R.J.G. (1994) 'Understanding clinical trials.' *British Medical Journal 309*, 755–6.

Salk, J. (1983) *Anatomy of Reality*. New York: Columbia University Press.

Saunders, K.B. (1994) Follow-up letter to Chock *et al.* 1994 in *British Medical Journal 309*, 1584.

Savitz, C. (1990) 'The double death: the loss of the analysit in the analytic hour.' *Journal of Analytical Psychology 35*, 241–60.

Schönberg, A. (1970) *Fundamentals of Musical Composition*. (eds G. Strang and L. Stein). London: Faber and Faber Ltd.

Schroeder, L.D., Sjoquist, D.L. and Stephan, P.E. (1986) *Understanding Regression Analysis*. California: Sage.

Searles, H. (1960) *The Non-Human Environment in Schizophrenia*. New York: International Universities Press.

Seymour-Smith, C. (1986) *Dictionary of Anthropology*. London: Macmillan.

Sheldon, T. (1994) 'Please bypass the PORT.' *British Medical Journal 309*, 142–3.

Shepherd, M. (1982) 'Karl Jaspers: General psychopathology.' *British Journal of Psychiatry 141*, 310–12.

Slattery, J. (1994) 'Tools may be blamed for shortcomings of workers.' *British Medical Journal 309*, 1158.

Smith, R. (1991) 'Where is the wisdom? the poverty of medical evidence.' *British Medical Journal 303*, 798–9.

Smith, R. (1992a) 'Audit and research.' *British Medical Journal 305*, 905–6.

Smith. R. (1992b) 'Promoting research into peer review.' *British Medical Journal 309*, 143–4.

Smith, R. (1993) 'Towards a knowledge-based health service.' *British Medical Journal 309*, 217–8.

Smith, R. (1994a) 'Filling the lacuna between research and practice: an interview with Michael Peckham.' *British Medical Journal 309*, 1403–7.

Smith, R. (1994b) 'Questioning academic integrity.' *British Medical Journal 309*, 1597–8.

Smythe, J.F., Mossman, J., Hall, R., Hepburn, S., Pinkerton, R., Richards, M., Thatcher, N. and Box, J. (1994) 'Conducting clinical trials in the new NHS: the model of cancer.' *British Medical Journal 309*, 457–61.

Stone, D.H. (1993) 'Design a questionnaire.' *British Medical Journal 307*, 1264–6.

Stott, N.C.H., Kinnersley, P. and Rollnick, S. (1994) 'The limits to health promotion.' *British Medical Journal 309*, 971–2.

Straus, E.W. (1966) *Phenomenological Psychology.* (translated in part by Eng E). London: Tavistock Publications.

Swinscow, T.D.V. (1990) *Statistics at Square One.* London: BMA Publications.

Sykes, R. (1994) 'Innovation in the pharmaceutical industry.' *British Medical Journal 309,* 422–3.

Thompson, S.G. (1994) 'Why sources of heterogeneity in meta-analyses should be investigated.' *British Medical Journal 309,* 1351–5.

Tognoni, G. Alli, C. Avanzini, F. Bettelli, G. Colombo, F., Corso, R., Marchioli, R. and Zussino, A. (1994) 'Need for rigorous assessment of clinical trials in general practice: lessons from a failure.' *British Medical Journal 303,* 969–71.

Turquet, P.M. (1974). 'Leadership: the individual and the group.' pp.337–71 in G.S. Gibbard, J.J. Hartman and R.D. Mann (eds) *Analysis of Groups.* San Francisco: Jossey-Bass.

Turquet, P.M. (1975) 'Threats to identity in the large group.' In L. Kreeger (ed) *The Large Group: Dynamics and Therapy.* London: Constable.

Van Maanen, J. (1988) *Tales of the Field: On Writing Ethnography.* Chicago: Chicago University Press.

Van Os, J., Galdos, P., Lewis, G., Bourgeois, M. and Mann, A. (1993) 'Schizophrenia sans frontières: concepts of schizophrenia among French and British psychiatrists.' *British Medical Journal 307,* 489–92.

Vernant, J-P. (1991) *Mortals and Immortals: Collected Essays.* (ed Zeitlin F.I.). Princeton: Princeton University press.

Warden, J. (1991) 'Patients' rights in research.' *British Medical Journal 303,* 1498.

Wheatley, D. (1992) Clinical trial results: whose responsibility? *Journal of the Royal Society of Medicine 85,* 242–4.

Whitten, P. and Hunter, D.E.K. (1990) *Anthropological Contemporary Perspectives.* Glenview Illinois and London: Scott Foreman.

Wickham, A. (1994) 'Minimisation.' *British Medical Journal 309,* 796.

Wilder, R.L. (1978) *The Evolution of Mathematical Concepts.* Milton Keynes: Open University Press.

Williams, S.M., Parry, B.R. and Schlupp, M.M.T (1992) 'Quality control: an application of cusum.' *British Medical Journal 304,* 1359–61.

Winnicott, D.W. (1972) *Playing and Reality.* London: Penguin Books.

Wright, R. (1993) *Caring in Crisis: A Handbook of Intervention Skills.* Edinburgh and London: Churchill Livingstone.

Yin, R.K. (1994) *Case Study Research: Design and Methods.* California and London: Sage Publications.

Index